Tiny Seeds

Sowing the Seeds for the Growth of Health, Wealth, and Happiness

Sherri Mahoney

Copyright © 2022 Sherri Mahoney
All rights reserved
First Edition

Fulton Books
Meadville, PA

Published by Fulton Books 2022

ISBN 979-8-88505-825-4 (paperback)
ISBN 979-8-88731-241-5 (hardcover)
ISBN 979-8-88505-826-1 (digital)

Cover photography credit to Katie Nemeth Photography
Edited by Sue Rasmussen

Printed in the United States of America

Introduction

This book is a product of thirty-five years of stories and work, collaborating with clients and discovering pieces of myself along the way. For years, people encouraged me to write a book of my own, but I felt the need to experience and learn things before I could write about them. The book I dreamed of writing would be built upon all the thousands of conversations and meetings with clients, and the words would pull us together like old friends while we would sit, talk, plan, and build a path to a successful future. The world is full of beautiful books written by many brilliant and talented people. That made it difficult to imagine I could contribute something to society that hadn't already been said—something different in a world already filled with so much noise and information. But a voice in my head told me that the stories and experiences I had to share were meant to be written and that readers, like my many clients, would welcome an imperfect voice calling out to tell them about a different path. This book has always been there, in the back of my mind. As the years passed and my list of stories and experiences grew, I finally felt like there was an abundance of information to share, and this book demanded to be written. The thoughts and ideas hungrily took up occupancy in every square inch of space in my mind, and I found myself crawling out of bed in the middle of the night to take notes so that things wouldn't be lost in the light of day. This book and its insights are my gifts to you. It's time to share the seeds I've collected so that you can grow your own beautiful life.

I've enjoyed an amazing career connecting with people and participating in their stories, and my own life has grown and changed alongside theirs. Years ago, I funneled my need to fix people into an accounting practice. Clients needing advice in all areas of their lives came steadily, and I loved helping them navigate their way through decisions and challenging times. When people shrugged at my career choice with the comment, "Better you than me," I smiled inside. The nature of the business I've grown has never been a path of misery or boredom. It was never just boxes and numbers; it was stories and people. The thousands and thousands of tax returns I've prepared over the years have all had faces and stories attached to them. Connections and relationships were forged as we met together in that private space behind my closed door. There were no boundaries, no limits on what was shared because when you enter a person's private financial world, those walls collapse. That's when relationships are built and stories are shared.

Life, I've discovered, is much like the work I do in my garden. It's not just about the seeds and the sun. You need to fortify and build the soil. Plants don't grow in desolate, barren soil, nor do they grow without the requisite amounts of sun and rain. Left unattended, weeds will overtake your garden and destroy your crops. On top of that, there are the bugs and other pests—opportunists that will consume and ravage your plants, ruining everything you've worked for in short order. Your work in the garden is never done. Our lives are like that; there is always more we can learn and perfect in our short lifetimes.

Most of us are not programmed for success. We've been thrown out into a cold field with broken compasses and seeds we don't know how to germinate. The growing seasons are short, and the winters are long. In order to reap the harvest we plant, we will need to dig deep, go back to our roots, and heal our broken parts. The journey to a beautiful life filled with health, wealth, and rewarding relationships is one that not all of us can travel. It is not a path for those not willing to do the work or experience some pain along the way. It is only for the strongest among us, but it is a life worth pursuing with all you can give. Are you ready to start the journey? Pour a cup of tea and pull up a chair; let's talk for a while.

Part 1

The Soil—Mending Your Beautiful Mind

Chapter 1

The World Is Full of Broken People

> Rock bottom became the solid foundation
> on which I rebuilt my life.
>
> —J. K. Rowling

The world is full of broken people. We are our harshest critics and worst supporters. Daily, we judge ourselves as too fat, too thin, too shy, and too loud. We worry about what other people think of us and compare our lives to those around us, finding ourselves lacking. Our minds are filled with anxious thoughts as we doubt and judge ourselves. The result of this vicious circle is the need to jumpstart our days with massive amounts of caffeine, dose ourselves with antidepressants, and put ourselves to bed at night with sleeping pills just to survive. Why are we all so broken?

Show me your typical American family with two and a half kids, wearing their designer clothes, with the perfect dog, the perfect house, and luxury sedans parked in the driveway, and I will show you the cracks in their story. Let's start with the parents. Were they valued as children, or did their own parents work too much and neglect them? Did their parents have unfulfilled dreams they tried to achieve by living vicariously through their children? Were one or both pawns as children batted back and forth like Ping-Pong balls as their parents tried to hold together a broken marriage? There are millions of ways that parents hurt their children, and these hurts and broken pieces are often the only tools at our disposal when we become parents ourselves. If you focus your gaze on a "perfect" family long enough, you will begin to understand that we are all made up of broken pieces. The delusion of a perfect family is one drink, one layoff, and one bad day away from it all falling to pieces.

> Adam came from the perfect American family. He was a star on the local football team, and his parents, both big sports fans, were super proud of him. In high school, a bad injury put him under medical care, and the coach and his father pushed for enough meds to keep him playing. Things went downhill from there. When the prescriptions dried up, he started using huge amounts of pot and then transitioned into a heroin dependency. They cleaned him up as best they could and shipped him off to college, where he met a nice girl who tried to balance out his moods and keep him off drugs. His mother struggled to understand his drug dependency. "Why is he like this," his mother would ask? "We have a beautiful home and a wonderful life. Why does he need to do these things?" His father kept just a little bit of cocaine in the safe that he used from time to time. He never had a problem knowing when to stop. Things continued to spiral downward for Adam, and he drove his car head-on into oncoming traffic but survived. It was either a thinly veiled suicide attempt or perhaps a cry for help. His mother told his girlfriend to get him under control. She would rather see him dead than be labeled as a drug addict. One cold December night, things took a dark turn, and he ended his life at the end of a short rope. At the funeral, his mother lay sobbing on the top of the casket over his dead body, crying out for her perfect, perfect boy.

Without a desire and a willingness to make a change, we run the risk of foisting upon our children the abuse and mistakes of the generation before us. Generational repetitiveness is the most popular path. Changing that path requires work, pain, and exploration. Most people will resist this path of change. We tend to choose the path of least resistance, and for most of us, this path is the same path our parents dragged us down.

Do you doubt you have broken parts? I spent my first year of therapy praising my perfect Laura Ingalls, Little House on the Prairie, childhood. My childhood was the only one I knew, and I had no compass to tell me it wasn't perfect. An abused child will almost always choose to stay with an abusive parent, even when given the option to go to a safer space. We choose what we know. We come into this world delivered into the waiting arms of loving parents who are slightly broken themselves. Imagine trying to build a house when all the tools you've been given to build with are broken. How strong will your foundation be if the cement isn't mixed properly? How straight will the beams be if your level is broken? Our parents do the best with the tools that they themselves were given. Unfortunately, the nourishment we suckle at our own mother's breasts is often tainted with all the regrets, resentments, failures, disappointments, and imperfections of her life. And so another generation begins.

How broken are you? There are obviously degrees of brokenness. Some people achieve huge financial success but make poor relationship choices that land them in one troubled relationship after another. Others I know claim to have wonderful long-term friendships and marriages but cannot seem to get ahead financially. Either way, something is still broken. A couple that starts out blissfully married but ends up with piles of debt, driving beater cars, and living in one of their parent's basements for years on end will eventually end up fighting about money. Quite often, you see the same people making the same bad choices and jumping into yet another unhealthy relationship, losing another job, and/or hitting up friends and family for money repeatedly. Some people are simply more broken than others. Are you willing to turn a magnifying glass onto the key areas in your life and identify a few that might need improvement?

Peter was born into a home with a narcissistic, alcoholic father and a mother forced to sacrifice the needs of her children to meet the father's demands. The oldest child struggled his whole life to overcome his need to fail, and the youngest followed the father's narcissistic, alcoholic path. Peter, the middle child, was broken beyond repair. He left a high-stress job only to be laid off from another one and then spent the next ten years unemployed. He simply could not find his way. Eventually, he ended up seeking in-patient treatment and spent his days heavily medicated. His own children parented him from one crisis to another, and he passed the time thinking of ways to end his miserable life.

- Can you identify some behaviors or patterns that don't serve you well?

- Do you have any broken parts?

- Are there areas in your life you would like to improve?

CHAPTER 2
Fixing Your Broken Bits

Gardening is the work of a lifetime: you never finish.

—Oscar de la Renta

Your mind is fertile ground. As children, we observe everyone around us, building our core values as we crawl at our parents' feet. When the values we learn as a child are false, we flounder as adults reliving the mistakes of our parents and mimicking their mastery of an unfulfilled life. What if our experience could be different?

Imagine a person dedicated to your healthy emotional development—someone separated from dysfunctional attachment, whose only motivation is to steer you toward unlimited success. Enter your therapist. Wally Lamb tells the story of a broken girl amazingly rebirthed by her therapist in his book, *She's Come Undone*. A therapist shines a light into the darkest corners of our minds, showing us the falsehoods we've adopted and helping us identify the truths that can set us free. A good therapist can help us recognize destructive behaviors and patterns, while a great therapist will parent us toward health in a way that our parents were unable to do.

In 1997, a friend referred me to a psychologist, a man named Porter, and I set up my first appointment. It didn't take him long to identify the word "victim" written in large letters across my forehead. I was going through a divorce at the time, and he helped me navigate those difficult waters and identify what had led me to such a destructive relationship. My childhood, I told him at the onset, was perfect—a mother who gardened and baked and an industrious, dependable father. He was smart enough to know better. Like an onion, we began peeling back the layers of my childhood, the falsehoods I adopted, my caretaking nature, and my attraction to narcissistic men. Therapy was a journey I relished. Eventually, I started dating a new guy, and Monday nights after my therapy, we would stay up for hours as he would extract as much information as he could about my session. Eventually, he found his own way through Porter's door. For twenty-five years, we have made the trek to Porter's door and left our baggage there to lighten our load. Sometimes, we've gone alone, sometimes together, and sometimes with gaps of months or even a year or two between our visits. He has taken two broken souls and made us whole. We have learned how to work effectively as a team, and when we hit troubled waters, we make our way back. At times, Porter has appeared almost mystical. His home is tucked under a canopy of pines, the ocean painting a portrait outside his windows. It is a lush paradise of exotic plants, and his persona mirrors the soul of the buddhas he collects. It's hard to place an age on him because he seems ageless in his grace, but given the years we've journeyed together, I know he must have passed his eightieth year. He declares himself to be a porter of people's heavy emotional baggage. A true Porter, he has gifted me with many years spent lightening my load through life.

Therapy is the key to opening the door to unlimited superpowers, and I've spent twenty-five years working with an amazing therapist as he parented me into a successful career and secure financial future. It's a journey I don't want to end, and it has given me the tools necessary to help my clients as they navigate their own lives. Clients are often looking for more than just basic tax preparation. There are tough decisions and troubled times to navigate, and healing my own soul has given me the ability to guide clients that have needed an outside voice.

My parents did their best, but the tools they had to work with were broken. They loved me, fed me, and clothed me, but they didn't have the tools to set me up for success. My mother fed me all her own fears baked into her finest apple pie. "You can't go off to college by yourself. Who do you think you are wanting more? You're a simple small-town girl. The world is a scary place. Stay here. Be safe."

> My mother was the oldest of twelve kids. One day, while she was outside keeping an eye on her younger siblings, a car pulled up. A man in a big car with a cigar hanging out of his mouth needed directions. The younger kids directed their gaze to her, the oldest, so she stepped forward and tried to tell him how to get to where he wanted to go, but he told her she needed to show him. She lived in a small town and didn't know enough to be afraid. He would pay her, he said. A mile or so down the road, he turned into a gravel pit and pulled her into the back seat, where he lifted her faded cotton dress and raped her. She was fourteen. He dumped her off by her house and threw a nickel out the window at her. The stench of his cigar hung in her hair and in her dress. She felt dirty and cheap. "Don't bother telling anyone," he said. "They won't believe you. You're nothing but a simple, small-town girl." She dragged herself home, broken and no longer trusting. Nobody

at home noticed her distress or cared about her silence. It was time for dinner, and there were a lot of mouths to feed. The shame she would carry on her journey through life had begun.

I recently got a text from a family member resistant to therapy. The picture shows a tall, alcoholic beverage being held up to the light. The caption written below reads, "All the therapy I need." An alcoholic always thinks the medication they need to stop the pain is in the next pour. Alcohol and pills, for many, are simply a Band-Aid to cover an open wound. The medical world has a pill for every ailment. Blood pressure too high? Take a pill. Cholesterol too high? They've got a pill for that. You say you can't sleep. Do your legs twitch when you get tired? Do you have stress and anxiety? Take a pill. Take a pill. Take a pill. Zombies don't just exist in the movies. People all around us are driving cars and operating equipment dulled on pills and jacked up on energy drinks. What if, instead, we listened to the messages our body is sending us and fixed the root of our problems? And why are we so intent on changing the feelings or symptoms we are experiencing? It's normal to grieve after the loss of a loved one; let yourself feel that loss. Depression is a symptom of our bodies asking us to look inward; take that look. Pain and illness are often a message that we need to modify things in our life; try listening to what your body is telling you. Change your diet, lighten your emotional load, and work through the issues that are the root of your stress and anxiety.

Paul and Debbie's daughter was excited but also nervous about heading off for her first year of college. Toward the end of her first semester, friends hooked her up with a doctor that could give her something to take the edge off. Her parents were happy that she was seeing a psychiatrist to help with her nerves, but then things took a dark turn. She became combative and would often call crying and distraught. One night, she called sobbing from a college party, and they could tell she had been drinking. They kept calling her cell but couldn't reach her. Eventually, her father made the trip to find her, but her college roommate said she hadn't been back to the room since early the day before. He scoured the area around her dorm and the location of the party for hours. Someone said they had seen a girl on a bridge, though, and the next day, her body was discovered. They found her cell phone on the bridge, and a review of recent calls revealed that she had called her psychiatrist repeatedly the night of her death. Paul reached out to the doctor, who confirmed that he had been treating her with a medication that had a side effect associated with suicidal tendencies. The doctor knew she had been suicidal, but privacy laws kept him from reaching out to anyone.

- What steps are you willing to take to discover and release any unhealthy patterns you have?

- Do you need to get some support in identifying the unhealthy patterns in your life?

- Is there someone you trust that can offer support in a healthy, nonjudgmental way?

- Are you willing to listen to the messages your body is sending you?

- Is therapy an option for you?

Chapter 3
Letting Go

We must be willing to let go of the life we've planned
so as to have the life that is waiting for us.

—Joseph Campbell

Finding ourselves requires that we let go of the ideas and falsehoods we've adopted that no longer apply to us or were never accurate. In my life, there were many things I identified with that were left behind in the ashes of my self-discovery. For years, there were limits placed on what I could accomplish and what I could be. I entered the workforce with a bright mind and a bucket load of ideas but no college education. My father bemoaned the life of the self-employed, declaring them all to be losers, living outside of society. Self-employed people had no self-control, health insurance, or retirement plans. I broke that convention when I started an accounting practice and then bucked it even further when I geared my practice toward educating and directing self-employed people toward the road to success. When I was struggling to find my path, there were voices in my head that said, "Who do you think you are, doing this on your own?" and "Don't forget, money doesn't grow on trees." It was hard to let go of the limiting thought that I couldn't grow a business of my own.

Early in my career, Beverly, my business coach, highlighted some destructive patterns in my way of functioning. I tended to delay making decisions, which often exacerbated an inconvenient situation into one that required me to take larger steps to put out a fire. For example, I would make excuses for an underperforming employee instead of making the decision to terminate their employment, even though the employee was not a good fit for me. My reaction time was too slow, and part of me craved the drama that would ensue. Once this behavior was exposed, I had the option to let it go. She also identified another destructive tendency when I described the annual three-month tax season as a period to be endured and suffered through. As a young woman with a long career ahead of me, she pointed out the sadness of suffering through so many months of my life. We identified strategies and systems I could implement that would make the tax seasons more enjoyable, and the decision to release another negative thought pattern was made. Letting go of learned or taught behaviors is not a path traveled by many, but if you can analyze your tendency to follow broken paths, you can identify newer ones that will bring a more beneficial result.

Often, we plow into adulthood with poorly written maps, planting our seeds in the same crooked rows as our parents and the friends we are aligned with. In school, children are taught how to do algebra, punctuate a sentence, spell, and read, but most will graduate without knowing how to balance a checkbook or file a basic tax return. We don't teach students about the hazards of credit card debt or the pitfalls of student loans. We learn about relationships both at home and at school, as we not only observe our parents fight about money, in-laws, and sex but also we witness the relationship dramas that circulate in the halls and classrooms. I can remember teachers that shared stories about their own broken marriages. One well-dressed teacher even bragged about how amazing it was to shop with credit cards. "It's no big deal," she said. "When the balances get too high, you just file for bankruptcy." How do we develop healthy maps when the people teaching us have not yet figured it out themselves? Over the years, I've had many clients who were teachers, and some of them were the worst I've seen at managing their own finances. Most of the college graduates I've hired with full accounting degrees cannot balance a checkbook, already have mountains of debt, and have never prepared a tax return. They've already planted their seeds in desolate soil with crooked rows.

We are constantly flooded with information, much of which is flawed or useless. Often these seeds of information take root in our minds; some seeds serve us well while others do not. Can you identify some thoughts or behaviors that work for you as well as others that could be replaced with better ones? Did you grow up hearing things like, "Money doesn't grow on trees," or "Money is the root of all evil?" Worse yet, perhaps you had to watch one of your parents suffer abuse at the hands of their spouse, only to be told that "Marriage is for life" and "You can't undo the bad choices you make."

> In Elizabeth Berg's moving novel, *What We Keep*, Ginny Young is traveling to see her mother, whom she hasn't seen in thirty-five years. Berg takes us on a journey back to Ginny's childhood, and we see the undoing of her parents' marriage and feel the pain of being abandoned by her mother. When Ginny finally makes the journey to visit her mother, we discover the agonizing choices her mother made, and we learn surprising truths about the people in Ginny's life. Truths that Berg, amazingly, has made us believe as well. We feel Ginny's surprise when she discovers that the facts she learned in childhood were not facts but falsehoods.

Rewrite your map. Identify the ideas and falsehoods that don't serve you. The challenge is in letting go of the things that hold you back while at the same time honoring and pushing toward the things in life that resonate as true. Letting go of limiting and false beliefs is the action necessary to make room for the healthier choices we must make.

- What lessons were you taught that no longer resonate as true? How have they impacted your life?

- Are there some negative patterns in your life you are ready to let go of? What might that feel like for you?

- Can you imagine replacing these negative patterns with positive, healthy choices?

- If you were to rewrite the map of your life, what would it look like?

Chapter 4
The Person Standing in Your Shoes

There are always flowers for those who want to see them.

—Henri Matisse

It's a story I've heard repeated many times over. "I need a better job, a better wife, or a better life." "There are just no good opportunities here." Clients disappear for ten years and then pop up again, complaining about the same problems. They have a different spouse but the same miserable life. Other clients will move three thousand miles away and then move back again, saying, "Life on the West Coast is even worse than life here on the East Coast." A client will max out their credit cards and then hit the bank up for a refinance to consolidate debt, only to max out their cards again a few short years later. Somebody will sell a house to liquidate debt and move to Florida, where they think they can live more cheaply, only to end up back in New England, living in their parent's basement a couple of years later. The answer, they boldly declare, is a different climate, location, or partner, but they make the same colossal mistake. They take themselves with them wherever they go. Let me repeat that. They take themselves with them wherever they go.

Happiness is a choice some people just can't seem to make. If we cannot be happy where we are today, then odds are a change of scenery won't make it better. In Hal Elrod's book, *The Miracle Morning*, he gives us a morning routine meant to maximize the potential in every day and tells us to put ourselves to bed with the promise that tomorrow will be a great day. These things alone won't guarantee that every day is an amazing day, but imagine what might happen if we let go of the idea that every day is destined to be a miserable day? The person you will spend more time with than anyone else in the entire world resides in you. Why not build this person into someone you enjoy spending time with? Try setting up your days for success. I make meditation and yoga a part of my mornings, and I've been doing it for many years because I know that the days when I make the time for these activities are my best days. We don't know what events might come to disarm our day, but setting ourselves up for success makes us more likely to manage things versus getting derailed.

> My mother died of ovarian cancer at the age of sixty-five, before she was able to enjoy her hard-earned thrift savings retirement plan. She spent her last Christmas at my brother's beautiful new home in Tennessee. My ex-sister-in-law had been unhappy in New Hampshire and dreamed that a new location, far away from all her mistakes, would bring happiness to her life. My mother was recovering after a round of chemotherapy and traveling to spend the winter in Florida when they stopped at my brother's house for Christmas. She was a petite woman with a compelling laugh, and aside from the occasional "dammit" or "shit," I rarely heard her utter an off-color word. My sister-in-law would sleep in every morning and then roll out of bed in the foulest mood. The prescription pill addiction she developed up north had followed her down south, and her moods ranged from bitterly unhappy to horribly miserable. Christmas morning, when she rolled out of bed in her typical unhappy mood, shouting and leveraging expletives at everyone in sight, including the dog, my mother, sick and dying, finally let loose with a litany that went something like

this, "If you can't haul your miserable fucking ass out of bed in the morning and put a smile on your miserable fucking face, there's something the fuck wrong with you." As the story goes, my father was so surprised that he dropped his coffee cup. My sister-in-law had moved a thousand miles away from her messed up northern life, but unfortunately, she had taken herself along.

Beginning in our teenage years, we spend much of our time trying to make ourselves appealing to other people. We develop behavior and appearances gauged to be desirable in the hopes of attracting the right people into our lives. Girls that were tomboys stopped playing with frogs and mud, and boys that liked cooking or drawing started working out. Our lives become about attracting and not being. Our focus shifts from listening to and experiencing life to learning how to be pleasing in the eyes of other people. Some people report that they lose themselves for years in the quest to attract the right mate or fit in, only to discover themselves again much later in life. Other people are so locked into their persona of being pleasing to the world that they will never relax enough to rediscover themselves. The pressures and images we absorb in our daily lives present us with intimidating standards for perfection, and we can run ourselves ragged trying to keep up with these unrealistic expectations. Society and the images of perfection we try to replicate in our own lives can make us harsh critics of our bodies and our lives. What if the eyes we used to judge ourselves were kinder and less judgmental? And what if we focused our energy on loving ourselves in spite of our imperfections?

The Farrah Fawcett hairstyle was popular when I was in high school, and every girl I knew spent hours trying to emulate it. I set my alarm for 3:00 a.m. every day when I would get up, perfect my Farrah hair, and then drop a specific hat onto the top of my head that would sufficiently flatten the hair while keeping the perfect shape. Keeping this hat on for a few hours after a spray of Final Net hairspray gave the style the holding power to get through the day. After styling, I would crawl back into bed for a few hours before getting up at 6:00 a.m. Maintaining this hairstyle was exhausting, and I would often fall asleep during study periods in school. Girls with curls were cursed in their attempts to flatten their hair to get the results, and I'm sure that when perms and curls had their day a few years later, they all breathed a sigh of relief. We were all obsessed with getting that certain look, regardless of whether it suited our hair or our tastes. Fitting in was the order of the day. The days of my wanting to fit in that badly are long gone, and I can't imagine crawling out of bed that early for something as silly as a hairstyle. I worry about my grandchildren, though, living in a world where everyone is posting and tweeting superficial images of perfection, and I applaud the actresses that are deciding to accept and share images of their gray hair and makeup-free faces.

Inevitably, life will find us all alone. Our children will grow up and leave our nest for lives of their own. The partner we connect with will eventually leave us through choice or death. We cannot spend every minute of every day in the company of others. Learn to find ways to bring joy into your life that aren't dependent on other people. Make yourself into someone you enjoy spending time with. Find simple hobbies that bring pleasure into your days. Be the person you want to take with you wherever you might go.

Trying to compete with the images we see on TV, social media, and in magazines is a recipe sure to bake a cake layered with disappointment. If you build a life based only on your ability to mirror the images you are being fed, you will never feel adequate. Learn and discover what your own style is. Decorate your home in a way that pleases your own eyes. Wear shoes that make your feet feel good and make walking pleasurable. And most of all, learn to love the person standing in those shoes.

- Have you ever tried to move away from a troubled situation or relationship to fix your life?

- Did things get better for you?

- Are there things you could do to attract more positivity into your life?

- What things could you do starting today to bring more happiness into your life?

- What kind of person do you want to be?

- What things can you do to become that person?

Chapter 5

Who's Your Daddy?

Storms make trees take deeper roots.

—Dolly Parton

Every family has its share of secrets, and mine is certainly no different. Growing up, I had a real father, Joe, and a stepfather, Al, whom I referred to as dad. I had two younger brothers born to my mother and stepfather, and they shared his last name. My last name, on the other hand, was long, difficult to pronounce and spell, and when the name-calling at school started, the boys had fun translating my awkward name into Miscofish. That wasn't the worst of things though.

As a young girl of three or four, I can remember my stepdad helping me put on my tights. He was crying, the only time I remember him crying, and I knew that I was going to visit my real father, Joe. The fact that this is one of my very earliest memories illustrates its significance. My visits with Joe were populated with circumstances that, years later, left me wondering why my parents would have ever let me visit with him.

Joe built and worked on race cars, so his weekends were spent in garages, and I can remember spending hours in a cold, unheated garage during many of my visits with him. Food and warm clothing were afterthoughts, so much of the weekend, I was left to my own devices, shivering and hungry on a cold garage floor. I can also remember having excruciating stomach pain on many visits, which I find interesting now, given that I have few digestive or stomach issues. Visits with Joe were punctuated with his reliance on booze and drugs, and when he picked me up, we went careening out of my driveway in his beat-up old Volkswagen van. We were almost always involved in some form of minor motor vehicle accident, where he would end up bumping into another vehicle or convenience store sign. After each mishap, he admonished me not to tell my mother, and like a good girl, I kept his errant driving to myself.

During one visit, we stopped by a mill pond where the water was covered with leaves. Mistaking the blanket of leaves for solid ground, I stepped onto them, falling into deep water. Joe stood by the side of the pond laughing while I floundered in the water until a passerby finally pulled me out. The memory still terrifies me, so I suspect I came close to drowning.

The sporadic weekend visits with Joe were a nightmare, and I was dumped off after the visits, starved and exhausted. There were often parties that went on until two or three in the morning that included his friends, who passed out and dragged themselves out in the morning. I would eventually crawl into my makeshift bed on the floor and put myself to sleep. I remember scrounging around in his kitchen, looking for scraps of food, but everything was moldy and full of bugs. Fathering a child wasn't high on his priority list, and keeping me warm and fed were goals that didn't even register on his scale. As I got older, the visits became more irregular. The rest of my family would often plan fun things like weekend camping trips while I spent hours perched on the back of the couch, staring out the picture window, waiting for Joe to pick me up. Time wasn't important to him, and quite often, he simply didn't show up. Eventually, I was smart enough to start making my own excuses, and the visits ultimately dwindled away to nonexistence. Unfortunately, they ended before my teenage years, when I might have welcomed the lack of parental supervision, but I was happy to be free from the chaos and near-death situations. My visits with Joe left me marked for life with a need to please and a fear of death that lies buried deep in my belly.

When I was twenty-nine, I was visiting one of my cousins. Out of the blue, she dropped a bombshell comment that the family rumor mill pegged me as not being Joe's daughter at all. They suspected Al was my real father all along. I scoffed at the idea, finding it too ridiculous to be true. Besides, what kind of parents would send a young, helpless little girl off to be with a man like that if they didn't have to? I let the idea percolate for a few years before finally mentioning it to my stepdad. "Yeah, well, we always assumed that was the case but thought you had probably already figured that out for yourself," he said. I was too shocked to speak.

The story goes that my mother realized she had made a bad choice marrying Joe. No shock there. As a young wife, her newly married older brother died when he suffocated under a pile of the earth when the ground collapsed as he was digging a well for his home. Joe wasn't around to comfort my mother as she grieved, but Al, a childhood friend who recently returned from his service in the Navy, was. My mother and her husband, Joe, welcomed a baby girl nine months later, and my mother's life of shame and secrets began to write a new chapter.

I always knew she adored me. She embroidered my name on all my little corduroy overalls, but I also wore an invisible coat sewn out of her shame. My stepdad suspected I was his daughter, but my mother was afraid to leave Joe. Finally, two years later, my stepdad smuggled my mother and me out of her bedroom window, where they escaped to begin their own life together. However, they maintained the pretense that Joe was my birth father. Apparently, losing both his wife and daughter in one blow would have been too much for the guy to handle. And so began my weekend visits.

A lifetime later, shortly after my mom's death, the phone rang in my office. It was Joe's sister, my aunt, calling to let me know that he had died. She was excited to have found me and said she had wondered about me over the years. Once again, I had doubts about the identity of my biological father. I called my stepdad to tell him about the news, and when I brought the subject up, he said, "I wouldn't touch that with a ten-foot pole." I asked him why he was so sure that he was my real father. He said he always figured Joe couldn't have children of his own. Two marriages and no kids meant that, obviously, Joe couldn't father a child. I told him I remembered Joe's second wife had a baby that died shortly after birth. My mother instructed me not to mention it when I visited with Joe because he and his wife were so upset about losing the baby. My stepfather's silence clued me in to realize that my mother had neglected to tell him about this baby. I could practically smell the doubt I had just planted in his mind over the phone.

Over the next few months, I became reacquainted with Joe's brothers and sisters, a family that I hadn't seen in many years, and it began to feel like a fit. They were all happy to have reconnected with me, and I couldn't bring myself to burst the bubble, especially since I really had no idea which man was my biological father. Once again, I'd been left holding the bag.

My husband was adamant. He said, "Show me a picture of both men, and I will tell you which one is your real father." I had an enlistment picture of four young men in their Navy uniforms. Two of them were candidates. "Hard to say," he said. "Any one of them could be your father." At that point, I decided it didn't matter who my real father was. I had a great stepdad who was always there for me growing up and another man who may or may not have been my biological father. It was time to move on. My mother, if she knew the answer, had taken this secret to her grave.

- Are there any unresolved issues from your past?

- Is there a way to resolve any of these issues?

- What things are you holding onto that are bringing you sadness?

Chapter 6

You Will Drop Your Basket

If a tree dies, plant another in its place.

—Carl Linnaeus

Odds are that despite our best intentions, life is sure to hit us in the gut from time to time. Show me a person who hasn't lost someone they loved, survived a breakup, or experienced an emotional drought, and it's likely that person is too young to have many life experiences. Even a person with the richest, most rewarding life has experienced hardship along the way. The tools and implements we keep at our disposal help us through these tough times and are the things that help us absorb life's punch to our gut. Some have been given better tools to cope, and others will need to find them on their journey through life.

COVID has proven to be an especially challenging time for everyone. September 11 was also a grim time. Events like this challenge our preconceived notions of how the world is supposed to function. In my lifetime, I never expected to see travel, restaurants, and stores across the world forced to close due to a pandemic. My eighty-year-old father never saw it in his lifetime either. Unprecedented challenges can cause even the strongest among us to drop our baskets.

> Bruce turned twenty-six in 2020, and life was in an upward swing. He was recently married, had just gotten a good job, had a great group of

friends, and had a lively social life. After months of being stuck at home during COVID, things started to fall apart. A deep depression began setting in. He couldn't seem to find anything to feel joyful about anymore. His friends stopped taking his calls when they got tired of his depressing, fanatical rants. After six months of his foul mood swings, his wife moved out, depressing him even more. She had suggested counseling, but he wasn't interested. The world was just one big shit show, and all the people around him were just a bunch of assholes. He had a difficult time getting to work, and his performance suffered; his boss eventually fired him. By early 2021, he found himself single, friendless, jobless, and homeless. He was left wondering how things had unraveled so quickly.

I had my own problems in 2020 and 2021. The summer and fall of 2020 had been difficult, listening to and helping clients make decisions as their businesses were impacted by COVID. However, I hoped that 2021 would bring normalcy with it. It was my thirty-fifth tax filing season, so things shouldn't have been that difficult. That assumption led me into several months of misery. For my entire life, numbers have always been solid, and I could always find logic in tax laws. Tax returns make perfect sense to me. Income is taxed once, and things that can be deducted are deducted once. Numbers always add up (one plus one will always equal two), and I love the sense and order that I can find in properly completed forms.

Per usual, my employees and I performed tax planning with our clients at the end of 2020. Those with businesses had received COVID-related business loans, and we did our planning based on treating them like normal business loans. When the 2021 filing season began, we started preparing taxes as usual. It didn't take long to realize we were in uncharted territory. Tax laws were being rewritten as we were filing returns, and returns that had already been filed were impacted. Clients sitting home watching their televisions were getting information faster than my national tax organizations, and the IRS could distribute it to tax preparers. Not only were COVID business loans being forgiven, but also the expenses paid with these loans were being allowed as business deductions. Tax laws no longer made sense. Our tax software was being updated sometimes a dozen times per day, so the results we were giving to a client one minute could be different a few hours later. Suddenly, one of the things that had always seemed the most solid, my faith in numbers, was being challenged. There were days I couldn't provide answers to the questions clients were asking, and I felt more powerless than I had ever felt when giving advice. The ground underneath us was moving as we walked across it.

The stories being shared by clients were also draining. One client lost both his parents to COVID; others were losing their businesses. A few restaurant clients had closed their doors, and many clients had been unemployed for months on end. I struggled to listen and advise, even though I was losing a little bit of myself every day. By the time tax season ended, I felt broken, both emotionally and physically. Sitting at my desk for so many hours each day had left me with chronic pain in my hips that made walking difficult, and my eyes, exhausted from the computer's glare, were sore and red. When it was over, I made an appointment with a naturopathic chiropractic doctor that helped to heal my tired body. It was clear I would need to reinforce my defenses before the next tax filing season.

> Twenty-five years ago, John and his best friend started a successful manufacturing company that employed fifty people. As clients go, John was one of my favorites. I admired his quiet assuredness, his sharp intellect, and he always seemed to have a great handle on things. COVID hit his company hard, and production was shut down repeatedly when cases among the employees were diagnosed. John was close to his workers and became anxious that they would bring COVID

home to their family members. His fears were realized when two elderly relatives of employees died of COVID-related conditions. The relationship between John and his friend began to deteriorate. The expense of payroll and their debt load demanded production, but the realities of COVID presented a different scenario. They could not agree on how to proceed. One day, John left work and drove away from it all. He left the business, his family, and his home. Months later, I learned more about John's story. Both his parents had died when he was young, and his childhood was spent living in a series of foster homes. As an adult, he struggled to maintain a strong facade by wearing a mask of success that cleverly hid his depression and anxiety. Ultimately, the load in his basket became too heavy to carry, and the garden he had planted in unfertile soil succumbed to the storm.

We will all be tested. Life does not guarantee the perfect amount of sun, rain, and pleasant weather. Amend your soil with the proper ingredients, and the seeds you sow will grow to become solid, strong plants with a better chance of weathering life's storms.

- What difficult situations have tested you?

- How did these situations make you feel?

- What is your method of managing stressful situations?

- Do these methods leave you feeling powerful or victimized?

Chapter 7
Misery Loves Company

The best way out is always through.

—Robert Frost

The tiny seed knew that in order to grow, it needed to be dropped in dirt, covered in darkness, and struggle to reach the light.

—Sandra King

A sad and challenging fact is that as we start to make healthy changes, there are people in our lives who may feel threatened. The positive changes we make can sometimes shine a bright light on the choices of others and cause them to question their lives. Often, these are the people in our circles who fear change the most.

One of the first things I learned in my own therapy was the crab pot theory, and every amazing self-help book I've ever read contains its own version. The version, as relayed to me, goes something like this.

The concept of crab mentality comes from the behavior of crabs in a pot. As one crab struggles to climb out of the pot toward a life of freedom, the other crabs climb on top of each other with the single goal of catching and dragging the escaping crab back into the bucket. Life is better for the crabs when they are all stuck in the same trap together. As a result, the entire pot of crab perishes. What's important to note is that people, like the crabs in the pot, through envy, jealousy, or competitiveness, will work together to destroy the escape of a single person trying to escape for a better future.

If you dare try to improve your future and move ahead in life, the people closest to you will sometimes resent and resist this change. My husband experienced this firsthand when he started his own therapy. His family hated his "bozo" therapist without ever having met him. "Why do you want to go and mess up your life like that with therapy?" they would demand. "You're fine just the way you are! So what if you are thirty years old, living with your parents, and on a direct path to bankruptcy? We don't see a problem here, so why do you?" His therapy was a threat to their own existence, and they were afraid of the changes that were sure to come.

> Kathy's son was the one driving the car when a drunk driver crossed into his path, killing his best friend in the passenger seat. With only one year of high school left, Kathy and her husband were intent on keeping their son on a straight path until he could get to college. His guidance counselor at school suggested he get counseling, but Kathy and her husband weren't those kinds of people. When one of his friends, who was also in the car, went to a therapist to talk about the accident, Kathy's son tagged along for a few sessions. When she found out about it, she was livid and threatened to sue the therapist for treating a minor without parental consent. "Stay away from my son," she ordered. "If my son has problems with the accident, we will deal with them on our own." That summer, Kathy and her husband took their son on a two-week European vacation where they all drank and partied their son's sadness away.

Sometimes, there is nothing more satisfying than sitting around with a group of friends, venting about our frustrations with coworkers, kids, and life partners. It's an out that we all need. However, spending too much time sitting around with the same group of people, bitching about how unfair life is, can get old pretty quick, and it's easy to get stuck in a rut. Some people will never get out of that rut. Sharing with friends is healthy, but (and this is a big but) you must be able to walk away from the conversation with a positive attitude. Ask yourself if these conversations are lifting you up or holding you down. Some people live for misery and drama, and they subconsciously create the chaotic world they live in. It's easy to get caught up in their drama, and they will encourage us to create conflict in our own lives. The next best thing to living in their own drama is living vicariously through ours. They will embellish, twist, and manipulate situations just to create drama in our lives to keep us aligned with their own miserable life. Remember, misery loves company, and creating drama is a tactic many people use to avoid dealing with life's realities.

One person's evolution toward a healthy existence can pose a threat, especially when the people around them have problems of their own they aren't willing to expose.

- Can you identify people in your life that resist when you try to make healthier decisions for yourself?

- How might your healthy decisions impact these people?

Chapter 8
Chaos and Drama Are Addicting

If you have good thoughts, they will shine out of your face like sunbeams, and you will always look lovely.

—Roald Dahl

I will not let anyone walk through my mind with their dirty feet.

—Mahatma Gandhi

My husband and I used to go out to dinner with another couple. Inevitably, by the end of the night, the wife was drunk, in tears, and her husband was whispering in my ear about how despicable his wife was. The last time we went out to dinner with them, the wife verbally assaulted a young waiter about serving her the wrong glass of wine. The surprised waiter had tears in his eyes by the time she had finished her tirade. After dinner that night, we both vowed we would never go out with them again!

Being around that much negative energy is draining and exhaustive, but for many people, drama and chaos are a way of life. The more they live it, the harder it becomes to contemplate living any other way. It becomes a normal pattern of behavior. What a miserable time suck!

Negativity is not a fertile ground for growing positive things. If the soil in your garden is sour, the seeds you plant cannot thrive! We all know toxic people like this. They attract drama, chaos, and negative attention and complain about their miserable lives every minute of every day. It's a drain. Other people are out there smiling, laughing, and living a beautiful life, while these people are locked in a never-ending storm of unfortunate events and circumstances. Is it possible they attract this negative energy? When you see the same people reliving the same nightmares over again, it's likely they aren't the innocent victims they want us all to think they are. It's not a stretch to conclude that the dramatic and chaotic lives they live manipulate the focus from the real problems they are afraid to address. It's easier to attack a stranger than take a good look at our own lives and relationships. Additionally, focusing on endless drama keeps us from dealing with our own addictions or mental health issues. Odds are that when you see someone creating countless dramas, they are merely crafting a distraction from the real issues. Toxic people will do anything to draw attention away from their own shortcomings, and all that negative energy they exude is bound to attract crappy situations.

As much as possible, move these toxic people away from the forefront or out of your life entirely. Life is much too short to let their negativity hamper your forward movement. Sometimes, things won't go your way. The steak you ordered won't be cooked the way you want, or the item you ordered won't arrive on time. When you are in an emotionally sound place, you can accept the reality of the situation. Certain people never get to that place.

> Ryan has been a client of mine through three different wives. His first wife was a train wreck—emotionally unstable and unable to care for her two children. When they divorced, he was granted custody of the kids. His second wife was just as bad. Social services took away her kid, and Ryan worked hard to help her regain custody. When she took off with another guy, she left her son with him. Luckily, he met another woman who was willing to move in with him and the three kids he was raising. It wasn't long before she

began to show signs of her own mental illness, but by then, she was pregnant with his child. She sought counseling for depression and was eventually put on disability. Ryan was thrilled to finally be raising a child of his own, but maintaining his new wife's mental illness was a full-time job. Then she got pregnant again. It was a difficult pregnancy, and the baby has some health issues of her own. His days are now spent traveling from doctor to doctor, taking care of his wife's illness. In the meantime, he's also dealing with all the kids plus the new baby, and it has become almost impossible to keep his job. He wonders why these things keep happening to him. He's a good guy with a decent job. How does he keep hooking up with these crazy women? He has five kids living with him and a wife that cannot even get herself out of bed in the morning to get them breakfast. Chaos reigns in his household.

Living in a constant state of drama or chaos is a suck of our limited, valuable time. We miss out on the simple pleasures of enjoying another person's company when we are fixated on feeling as though we are being slighted or we are locked in instigating a dramatic battle. Sometimes, we create our own drama. My formative years left me craving a constant state of chaos, and it was an addiction that I struggled to break. When I was younger, I can remember delaying paying my car insurance or car payment right up until the due date. Inevitably, I would end up with late charges or receive cancellation notices. A spat with customer service would ensue where I would have to make my case that the check was in the mail or had been mailed on time. Obviously, the fault for its non-timely receipt had to rest on someone else's shoulders. It didn't take me long to figure out that I was the one creating these situations and that I could just as easily find something more productive on which to spend my valuable time. Ultimately, my dreams for success had to take precedence over my need to create drama, and I've stopped building fires that take too much energy to extinguish.

>Former clients Marcia and her husband Bob wanted to talk about everything except their taxes when we got together. They insisted on meeting frequently because there was always a new financial emergency that needed to be discussed, and they spent most of their time with me arguing amongst themselves. It was exhausting! Their arguments were so petty that I found it difficult to think that they even believed their own point in the dispute. Every time we met, they were caught up in yet another family drama. It was impossible to keep track of who they weren't speaking to and what new lawsuit they were involved in. Marcia's father was so mad at her when he died that he cut her out of his will right before his death. She then sued her brother to try to get a piece of the inheritance. Ironically, the year before he died, her father had also cut Marcia's brother out of the will. Now Marcia was trying to figure out what to do because she was counting on her father's inheritance for her own retirement. Her husband's side of the family isn't much better. He has two sisters he doesn't speak to anymore, and he's in the middle of a custody battle between his niece and his sister. Marcia and her husband have three grown children, but none of them can get along. She blames it all on their spouses. Every time I see Marcia, she cries and asks me why can't everyone just get along? From the outside looking in, it looks like those apples didn't fall too far from the family tree. I finally figured out that this couple wasn't looking for tax help. They were looking for someone to listen to them whine about their family drama.

In my work, patterns present themselves. The same clients come back year after year, and some of them have been with me for over thirty-five years. That's long enough to identify patterns that repeat themselves in generations. The son of a client will come in, and I will notice the same style of handwriting or the same type of ledger sheets. The methods they use to organize their paperwork or the way they document their tax payments will seem eerily familiar. We learn a lot from our parents. They teach us many wonderful things, but we pick up a few of their unhealthy habits as well. Show me a client feuding with everyone he meets, and I will show you that client's kid following along in his father's footsteps. The problem for all of us is identifying the behaviors that we've learned and deciding which ones to keep and which to release.

None of us know how many seasons we have left on this earth, but we do have some control over how we spend our time and who we spend our time with. How do you want to use the time you have left, and which people lift you up and inspire you to live your best life? Cultivate these relationships. Maintaining relationships with toxic people will keep you in the crab pot. The wealthiest people among us cannot buy more time when theirs is up, so pay attention to the value of your time. My mother died when she was sixty-five and never got to experience the promise of her great retirement. Our time here on earth is composed of an undetermined number of hours, days, weeks, and years. Time is one of the few things that can't be manipulated or extended. Sure, a good diet and healthy lifestyle might get us a few additional years, but there is no guarantee. Imagine your life measured with grains of sand in an hourglass, and as each piece of unrecoverable sand drops, you lose an hour. Now imagine making a choice to fill those hours and days with moments of joy and love. The choice is yours to make.

- Are there any toxic people in your life?

- What things can you do to minimize your contact with them?

- Do you create any drama or chaos in your own life?

- What things could you do to avoid drama and chaos in your life?

- Are there situations in your life that you avoid by creating the distraction of drama?

Chapter 9
The Mind-Body Connection

Our bodies are our gardens. Our wills are our gardeners.

—William Shakespeare

Our bodies are the victims of the transgressions of our minds. Do you believe that you can worry yourself to death, work yourself sick, or die of a broken heart? I've seen it firsthand. The mind/body connection is powerful, and if we're not careful, issues that aren't dealt with in a healthy manner can manifest as an illness. If we avoid addressing difficult situations, stay in an abusive relationship, or consistently ignore other problems in our life, these things will eventually find a way to get our attention by making us sick. Our immune system is compromised and doesn't work to its fullest capacity when we are tired and stressed. It only makes sense that when our minds are contaminated with fear, anguish, or pain, our body eventually pays the price.

> Ralph was a client that came to me with quite a tax problem. He hadn't filed tax returns in over ten years. He said that the first year, he just forgot to file, and then things started to snowball. The more the years began to stack on top of one another, the more ashamed he became about reaching out to anyone for help. By the time he came to see me, his weight had dropped to 150 pounds. He wasn't sleeping at night and

had developed a severe case of eczema, which his doctor thought might be stress-related. We developed a plan to deal with the late filings and began checking them off one at a time as they were completed. It took time to collect the documents and complete the filings, but six months later, he was sleeping again, gaining weight, and his eczema had disappeared. Now he's one of the first clients to get his documents in at filing time.

Some people will identify and remedy the issues that are causing their bodies pain. Unfortunately, other people will never get there.

Philip was a difficult client, always filing at the last minute, but I still enjoyed working with him. He would always come in with a big smile, a hug, and a promise of chocolate or a bottle of wine if I squeezed his return in. It was hard to resist his charm and his smile, and I always found the time to get his taxes done before the deadline. He was self-employed but never made his estimated payments. He never complained about the tax balance he owed and told me that he was headed straight home to sign the returns with his wife, and they would be in the mail that night with a check for the full amount of the tax. It was early in my career, and I was naive enough to believe him. One day, Philip stopped by my office. He gave me an especially big hug and told me he was dying. He had just been diagnosed with cancer, and his doctor said he didn't have much time, so he was letting the people in his life know. I was surprised and told him that surely there was something they could do and that hopefully, the treatment they were trying would buy him more time. He said he didn't think so. I noticed a yellowish tint in his eyes that made me believe him, and sure enough, he passed just a few weeks later. Months later, I received a call from his daughter, who had discovered a shocking situation. After her father's death, they had found boxes containing notices, bills, and demand letters from the IRS. Over the years, her father had amassed hundreds of thousands of dollars of tax debt and had managed to keep it hidden from everyone, including his wife and family. In an elaborate deception, he had opened a separate post office box for tax mailings, filed tax returns and dodged the tax collection for years. His wife was trusting and had always left their tax situation to him. His daughter was working as a certified public accountant for a firm in New York and couldn't believe that she had seen no signs of his tax problems. I confessed that I was just as surprised. Philip was popular in the community and had held several elected positions in town. He was respected by many for the successful business he had built. When he left my office, he would joke about the checks he would have to write to pay the tax, but I never doubted him when he said that he was going home to write out those checks. We were all victims in his ruse, but I've always felt that he was the biggest victim. I can't help but feel that he knew he was running out of time before his debt was discovered, and I think the shame would have been too much for him to bear. His body finally provided him with the exit he needed from the disaster he had created.

Funny how our minds lock onto important moments in our life. I remember standing in my kitchen as the sun started to set. I was washing vegetables at the small sink on our kitchen island the day my mother called to tell me the doctor was sending her for additional testing. Frustrated with her own doctor, who was dismissing her symptoms and knowing that something felt very wrong, my mother had gone to the yellow pages and made an appointment with a gynecologist. That moment as water ran over my hands, time stood still, and I held my breath. I did my best not to let her know I was scared. "You don't know for sure," I said. But she knew. She was sixty-three and just starting her retirement. She hadn't been in a rush, though, to start enjoying her days. Like us, she thought she still had plenty of time. After all, her own mother was in her nineties and still going strong.

In the last couple of years prior to her death, my mother and I had been discovering each other in a new phase of our relationship. My therapist had encouraged me to explore my past with my mother, and she was receptive and looking to share stories from her life. She shared her story of having been raped at fourteen and the shame that had kept her silent for all her years. We discussed her marriage to Joe and her affair with my stepfather, Al—another source of shame in her life that she had locked in a box and thrown away the key. It was a relief to finally talk about it after so many years, she said. She wondered about the impact of holding onto such horrible things for so long, and we talked about her worries and fears that she transferred onto her children as she parented. She told me how proud she was of the business I had started—something she wouldn't have been brave enough to undertake. I was looking forward to my mother's retirement and seeing her transition into a state of relaxation. Her job had kept her busy working for so many years. Her cancer, though, had other plans, and she died when she was sixty-five, after two rounds of chemotherapy. I often wonder about the irony of the ovarian cancer that attacked the part of my mother's body exactly where the source of her greatest shame had lain buried for so many years.

- Can you identify times in your life when you were run down or tired and your body responded in a negative way?

- How do you think our body responds to negative or painful situations in our lives?

Chapter 10

Stop It! Buried Alive in a Box

We are all just prisoners here, of our own device.

—The Eagles, "Hotel California"

Life demands that at some point in our lives, we pull up our big adult pants and get the fuck on with it. Get the therapy, confront those who have harmed you, beat the crap out of a pillow if you need to get rid of some anger, and inevitably, you need to own your own shit. We cannot blame our faults, failures, and every single mistake we make on the horrible things that happened in our past.

There is a long list of hugely successful people that experienced trauma in their lives—Oprah Winfrey, Demi Moore, Jim Carrey, Charlize Theron, to name just a few. Our lives are all about our choices, and we can make a choice to let our past break us or make us. A cat will always land on its feet. Whatever life throws at you, put your feet down, dig your heels in, and master the landing. Land on your feet. You can spend your entire life whining and complaining about the abuses you've suffered and the bad lessons you've been taught, or you can make the decision to take another road. This less-traveled road will be unfamiliar at first, and it will take everything you have to take that first step but do it.

There is a hilarious Bob Newhart comedic skit you can easily find online. A woman goes to see Bob, a psychiatrist. He tells her he charges five dollars for five minutes and absolutely nothing after that. He does no insurance billing and guarantees that the session will not last the full five minutes. Full payment in cash is required at the time of service, and you must have the exact amount of cash on hand. He does not make change. She confesses her fear of being buried alive in a box. He gives her two magic words, guaranteed to fix her problem. "Stop it!" he shouts. He asks, "Do you want to go through life being scared of being buried alive in a box? That sounds frightening. Then, stop it!"

"But it's been with me since childhood," she says.

"We don't go there," he says while continuing to shout, "stop it!"

"I'm bulimic. I stick my fingers down my throat. I have self-destructive relationships with men. I'm afraid to drive," she says.

"Stop it, stop it, stop it!" he shouts. "Don't be such a big baby." Finally, he gives her ten words that he thinks will clear everything up for her. "Stop it, or I'll bury you alive in a box!" he shouts.

The skit is meant to be funny, but the reality is harsh. When you give your life away to the transgressions of your past, you are choosing to bury yourself alive in a box. Many believe there is a hell and that it exists here on earth in the things we do to ourselves. Stop luxuriating in your broken past and blaming all your mistakes on something that happened long ago. Stop it! It's time to crawl out of the box.

- What negative ideas and patterns are you holding on to?

- Are you ready to let go of some negative things in your life and replace them with some positive behaviors?

- Can you stop letting the negative thoughts and behaviors in your life run the show?

Part 2

Planting the Seeds for Success

Chapter 11

Make Happiness a Priority

Never put off planting something or you will find that ten years later, you are saying, "If only we had planted that wisteria," and you are filled with sad thoughts. It isn't too late. Do it now.

—A. A. Milne

The foolish man seeks happiness in the distance.
The wise grows it under his feet.

—James Oppenheim

Losing my mother at a relatively young age changed many things for me. My mother was always waiting to start living her best life. I remember one time shortly before she died, she went out for lobster rolls at Red's in Maine. She had read about the famous Red's Eats in Yankee Magazine and was so excited, but she would only let herself eat half of the lobster roll. There would be plenty of time for more lobster, she said. Three months later, she died, so there really wasn't any time for more lobster.

In my early twenties, I read the book *The Road Less Traveled* by M. Scott Peck. The chapter about delayed gratification resonated with me. I always saved the frosting on my cupcake for last. My mother taught us to work first and play later. She resisted giving herself nice things. Scrimp and save today so that you can play later was her message. All the clothing she bought came off the clearance racks, and she made do with her old furniture and chipped dishes. She was saving all her money for her retirement years. She drove us all with the mantra to work hard now and play later. For her, there was no later.

When my husband first came into my life, he surprised me with his "play now, play later, play every day" mantra. But the dishes, the laundry, the dusting, the work that needed to be done gnawed at me. We were opposites, pulling in two very different directions. He challenged my belief that every day had to be about work first and play later. The problem with my belief, I discovered, was that my days often ended with no time to play. The problem with his belief was that by the time he was finished playing, there was no time for work, and his often overdrawn checkbook reflected that lifestyle. It took years for us to learn how to navigate through these different belief systems and come to a healthy resolution.

My mother's death brought home the realization that life could not be squandered entirely on work without making time for happiness or play. She died before getting the opportunity to spend her hard-earned retirement savings. All the places she had dreamed of seeing, the exciting things she wanted to do, and the little luxuries she denied herself were never hers to experience. Death robbed her of those things.

Life after my mother's death made me greedy for happiness all the time. Sunsets, walks, and time with family and then grandkids suddenly became more important than just working and saving for a rainy day. *What if there is no rainy day?* the voice in my head would ask. My husband had always dreamed of owning a boat, and shortly after my mother's death, I began to entertain the idea. My need for light and happiness became a strong opposition to all my fears. We found an old boat with two large inboard motors that had been sitting on the hard (out of the water) for two years. One of her motors was blown. We made a ridiculously low offer, and suddenly, we were boat owners. We spent that spring replacing her blown motor, rehabbing her old and tired systems, and we launched her that summer. Slowly, my fear of being on the water began to lessen, and I started to enjoy the rhythm of the water. Being lulled to sleep at night by the gentle rock of the boat soothed my soul. My mother never let herself enjoy such happiness. She was saving it all for a retirement that she would not live to enjoy.

> Rick and Marcia came to me in their mid-sixties. He had been working his whole life as a self-employed landscaper, and she stopped working at a young age to raise their children and help him in the business. Rick wasn't much on giving away his hard-earned money to the government, so he had made sure to keep his taxable income pretty low every year. They also liked the nicer things in life. Marcia always drove a Mercedes, and Rick had a lineup of big trucks and lots of landscaping equipment. He argued that they were always tax deductions. Life had been good for a long time, with great vacations and a beautiful home. They always carried lots of debt, but they had a certain image they wanted to maintain. Everything they owned had to have a designer label or portray their image of success. It was always about having the right shoes, clothes, and a home that made it look like their life was successful, even though their bank account reflected a different story. They lived their lives behind a curtain of smoke and mirrors. They both had parents that died young, so they weren't sure they would see their own retirement years. They just never expected it to come up so fast, but now they were worried. Rick had hoped one of their boys would take over the business, but both sons had run far from the family business to other parts of the country. They have no retirement funds, and since their taxable income has always been so low, their social security is a fraction of what they need to live on. Rick doesn't think he can work much longer.

Working with clients has brought this struggle to my desk on dozens of occasions. I have had many clients so reckless with money that they become a burden to their children. I have also met clients so intent on saving for their future that they deny themselves the most basic happiness.

The challenge I have found is in the balance and finding that just-right balance will challenge us all. Living a financially reckless life with no savings for retirement is hapless and irresponsible. This type of behavior will render us dependent on our children or other family members for financial support, which they will resent. On the other hand, spending our entire lives saving and denying ourselves happiness each day is a gamble we can't afford to take.

Oliver is one of the sheep on our farm. At our lavender event in 2020, we had over six hundred people attend, with some traveling from quite a distance. It was mostly because of Oliver and the photo of him as a small lamb in the lavender fields that went viral on Facebook. The picture continues to get lots of likes and comments on social media. The picture is so fabulous that I had it framed, and a copy hangs in my office where I can look at it every day. My friend, Katie, is an amazing photographer, and her photos of animals and farm settings have earned her quite a reputation. Unlike many sheep on our farm that move onto other farms or into the freezer, Oliver has managed to keep his home. Oliver was the last lamb born to my oldest sheep, Eve, who has since passed away. At birth, he was frail and weak and had difficulty standing, so I held him while he nursed until he could stand on his own. We have a bond, but the thing I love most about him is the joy he exhibits every morning when I walk into the sheep pasture with the morning feed. Oliver bounces, jumps, and flips for joy on the way to the feed station every single day. There are eight sheep and two donkeys that will all take their place at the feeding bin and vie for a few mouthfuls of grain, and Oliver's portion will be small. None of that matters to him though. Every day that he gets just a bit of grain and a portion of hay is a great day for him. His needs are simple and easily met.

Happiness doesn't have to come with a steep price tag, and sometimes, it's as simple as vanilla ice cream. Find the balance. Create moments of joy every day, and remember to keep an eye toward the future at the same time. Put a little bit of whatever you have in each basket and eat the ice cream. Eat the whole damn lobster roll, for that matter.

- What moments of joy do you make time for each day?

- Are there things you can do to find more happiness in your days?

- Are you investing in your future?

- What changes are you willing to make to save more for your future?

Chapter 12
Living Your Best Life

In the spring, at the end of the day, you should smell like dirt.

—Margaret Atwood

Give every day the chance to become the most beautiful of your life.

—Mark Twain

Watching and collaborating with people has taught me a lot. It's usually the same story—people wondering why they are still doing the same old things and stuck in the same job with no changes coming their way soon. Unfortunately, most of these people can't seem to find their way out of this rut.

If you want different results, you will need to change how you are doing things. Identify the things in your life that aren't working and consider if there might be some things you can change to generate different results. There are plenty of things in life outside our control, but there is one person we can control. Start with the only person you can control—*you*!

Many years ago, I dated a guy, John, who wore T-shirts that read "It's hard to soar like an eagle when you're surrounded by turkeys." He liked the saying so much that he had different colored T-shirts made for every day of the week. He constantly compared his performance to workers around him and judged them to be too slow or less skilled than he was. John wanted a supervisor's position but was continually passed over for promotions. He blamed the turkeys he worked with for his failures, never stopping to realize that his lack of compassion and the constant judgments he made of his coworkers were traits that would have limited his abilities to be an effective supervisor. Unfortunately, John was the one behaving like a turkey.

My husband has owned a plumbing business for many years. Finding good employees is one of his biggest challenges. He has a ten percent theory that I have consistently found to be true. Only ten percent of people are putting forth their best. Ten percent of employees are getting to work on time and doing their best at their job every day. Ten percent of people are the best in their field; the rest are just getting by. Look at any field of work, whether it's doctors, plumbers, builders, or accountants. Let's take the example of one hundred plumbers. Out of those one hundred plumbers, only ten percent or ten of those plumbers are amazing.

What group would you want to be in? Which plumber do you want in your house? There are plenty of people doing just enough to get by every day, putting in as little effort as possible, and wondering why they aren't getting the one hundred percent results they want.

The people getting the one hundred percent results are giving more than just minimal effort. They are fortifying their bodies and minds so that they can give one hundred percent of what they have to offer every day. Do you doubt this? One of the most consistent character traits of extremely successful people is that they are early risers, and many successful people have morning regimes that include yoga, meditation, or exercise. Your body is a machine. If you want premium performance, you must support it with the resources it needs to function at its highest level. Nourish your body and mind, and your body will provide you with the machine you need to operate at one hundred percent. Do you want to ask your boss for that raise or take your business to the next level of success? Try giving one hundred percent instead of the minimum required effort and watch your life change.

> One day, I discussed a situation with a client. Pat was upset about her brother, who had been unemployed for over eight years while he searched for

the perfect management job. "What's the matter with him?" she asked. "Doesn't he understand that work isn't supposed to be a good-frigging time? Nobody is getting up in the morning, pulling on their socks, and rushing out to get to work with a smile on their face. People don't go to work because they like going to work. My husband despises his job, and that's the way life works. Work is what you suffer through every day to pay the bills." The picture of her husband suffering throughout his days saddened me, and I wondered about the future of her children having that be a lesson in their lives.

From day to day, you will find that your best will be different. Sometimes, we just aren't where we want to be physically or emotionally, but the thing to keep constant is that each day, we do our best, whatever that might be. There are days when I check off everything on my list and other days when a computer glitch or complex tax situation will take hours to resolve, leaving me with the sensation that I am spinning my wheels. Sometimes, I'm just plain tired or run down, especially during an intense tax season. We all have periods in our lives when difficult situations with children, spouses, illnesses, parents, or other stresses in our lives distract us, but every morning presents a new opportunity to do our best. I read a little book many years ago by Don Miguel Ruiz titled *The Four Agreements*. I read this book yearly and learn from it every time. The fourth agreement in this book is to always do your best. It's an outwardly simple challenge that many people will never attempt. If you approach each day with the intent of doing your best, you will rise above the people only willing to do enough to just get by. Going to bed at night with the satisfaction that you did your best puts your mind in the right place to be ready for tomorrow's opportunities.

In my business, I've seen too many people squandering days or years waiting for the inheritance, the big raise, the winning lottery ticket, the divorce, or some other big life event that will *happen to them* to finally allow them to live the life they deserve. Did you read that previous sentence? They are waiting for an event to happen to them! While those people are sitting on the couch waiting for the life of their dreams to fall out of the sky into their cookie-crumb-filled laps, other people are out there making those wonderful lives happen. If you want to live your best life, you need to be the one plowing that field and planting those seeds. A great life is something that is carefully cultivated. It's not an event or circumstance that happens to you. It's a plan and design that is carefully grown and tended and finally harvested.

Living our best life requires that we do our best not only in our work or business lives but in our relationships as well. It's far easier to listen with half an ear than it is to actively listen and engage in a conversation. One of my past tendencies was to keep typing or working on a task on my computer while on the phone with a client. I've learned that spinning my chair so that my view is out the window instead of trying to listen and work at the same time allows me to better participate and respond to my client's questions. It took a few unfortunate pauses in a client's conversation for me to understand that my multitasking was apparent to the client on the other end of the phone. Clearly, I wasn't putting my best self into the conversation.

It's also easy to let our emotions drive our words or actions rather than think past the instant gratification or satisfaction to be had by airing our anger. Have you ever lashed out in anger only to wish that you had thought a little before reacting so harshly? Living our best life requires that we stop and wonder what impact our words will have on the relationship. Text messages and social media make it too easy to wound other people. The problem with these forms of communication is that we are physically distanced from the people we are in the exchange with. It is easy to misinterpret a text when you can't see someone's eyes or read their body language. The distance alone means that we are functioning in a vacuum, not having to deal with the immediate reaction of someone's emotional response. You can decide to use these forms of communication to spread happiness and love, or you can use them to spread emotional pain. The next time you want to send a nasty text, try picking up the phone and having a conversation. A conversation is a tool that allows for an exchange of ideas, and sometimes, all we need to do is listen to the other person's perspective or the pain in their voice to know that what the situation really needs is communication. I'm guilty of sending a few of my own angry texts. Hindsight makes me wish I would have reconsidered my options.

Living your best life is vital because it invites wonderful things into your life. Open your mind to doing your best every day, express yourself in a loving way, and the life you want will grow from the tiny seeds you have planted.

In the following chapters, we are going to identify what your best life looks like. Are you willing to give one hundred percent to get that life?

List these things in order of importance:

- Family

- Relationships

- Wealth

- A home

- Hobbies

- Travel

- Health

- Possessions

Chapter 13

Stop Suffering through Your Days, Your Jobs, and Your Life

Wherever life plants you, bloom with grace.

—French proverb

Are you blooming, or are you suffering? Our bodies weren't deposited onto this planet to suffer. We were delivered here to discover, to grow, to bloom, and to participate in the cycle of life. Our time here is nothing more than a tiny seed cycling through our season of growth, life, and death. Do you want to spend that one season in misery?

Every day gives us an opportunity to experience and find joy. We all wake up on the same day, and we are given the same options. We can either get out of our beds and see the beauty in the sun rising, or else we can look out that same window with a predisposed attitude about the shitty day we are about to have. We might get in our cars and head to work, only to hit every single red light and then find a line at Starbucks twenty cars deep. Is that a shitty day or an opportunity to spend a little more time in the warm bubble of our car listening to great music? I've sworn at cars that have cut me off, cursed the long lines, and stressed about being late. Not every morning starts the way I'd like. For example, take the relatively simple task of feeding the sheep and donkeys on our farm in the morning. There are days I come close to getting trampled, splattered with chicken poop, or falling on my ass in the slippery mud. However, it brings me joy on most days when I slow down and observe the animals' excitement over their breakfast. I've learned to find and take pleasure everywhere I can.

Our jobs are what we contribute to our world and our community. For ten years, I taught business development classes to entrepreneurs that were starting their businesses. One of our tasks was to identify and connect the business owner to the value of the product they were bringing to the marketplace. As a plumber, my husband installs state-of-the-art mechanical systems. He's not just installing a heating or cooling system. He's bringing warmth into a cold home or cooling air into an uncomfortably hot environment. He's selling comfort. And don't we all want comfort in our homes?

Years ago, I had an employee that had given up plans to become a child advocacy lawyer to focus on accounting. After a short time, we parted ways. She told me she just couldn't see any value in preparing tax returns and simply putting a bunch of numbers in boxes when there were children suffering in the world. I was happy to see her move on because she had failed to identify the value in the service we were providing. We weren't just putting numbers in boxes or handing over a stack of tax forms. I don't do tax returns for the joy of telling people they must fork over their hard-earned money to the IRS. Our job is to take a difficult situation that most people find intimidating and eliminate the fear and stress. We educate people on their tax situation and work on ways to reduce their tax liability. We solve other people's tax problems. Along the way, we guide, advise, and help people find a healthy path toward financial success. Hardly a trivial job and certainly not a job without value!

Mike Rowe hosts the show *Dirty Jobs*, and he's seen plenty of the world's dirtiest jobs. The people in these dirty jobs have some serious cause for complaint, but Mike always finds humor and value in these jobs. Mike has learned a lot in his years making this show, and it's given him a platform to question how we discount and look down on the people doing these dirty jobs. If you want to eat meat or drink milk, someone must inseminate the cows and milk or butcher them. We need people to keep our sewers flowing and our waterways clean. We've placed so much value on a college education that there are generations of people with advanced degrees who demand all these services but don't recognize their value, and furthermore, they often demean the very people providing the services. Where would we be without the tradespeople or service providers that keep our homes safe and our world running? We've lost sight of the value these people bring to the world, yet we need them to make our lives work.

> Pat called one day to get some numbers for the financial aid forms she was completing for her son. She was in a foul mood. "He's thinking about throwing his life away on a teaching degree," she said. "I told him that I didn't spend the last ten years of my life doing his homework and medicating his ADD ass through school so he could settle for an underpaid teacher's job. Besides," she said, "your father has spent his whole life suffering away his days at a job he hates, just so he can give you the education you deserve." She later told me her son had finally "come to his senses" and decided to pursue the law degree she had suggested.

When COVID shut the world down in 2020, everyone sitting in their high-rise office buildings went home and stayed there for months. They were not essential workers. They were not considered necessary to keep our world functioning. Do you know who kept working? The builders, plumbers, electricians, and other tradespeople. You know who else didn't go home? The frontline medical workers and emergency responders and the farmers that grow our food. There were no shutdowns for these people. The average age of a plumber in Massachusetts is fifty-five. Young people don't want these jobs because we've taught them that these jobs aren't valuable. They are challenging, and you could end up with dirty hands and calluses. I have hundreds of clients with kids racking up hundreds of thousands of dollars in student loan debt for business degrees and only a few encouraging kids toward work in the trades, farming, or service industries. Trade jobs and service jobs pay well and offer a bright future. They offer an individual the opportunity to build or create something. These are satisfying jobs that provide valuable services.

One of the most notable animals in our barnyard is a turkey named Tom. He's lived on our farm for over four years, managing to avoid both our Thanksgiving table and the coyotes that often hunt our barnyard birds. As a heritage turkey, he's fancy in his own right; but when he fans his entire tail of feathers, he can't compare to the beautiful blue indigo peacock that also calls our barnyard his home. Tom's feathers are a common brown, and his tail, less than a quarter of the size of the peacock's tail. But nothing can keep him from shining. Every single day, he fans out his tail, pumps himself up, prances, and dirty dances his way across the barnyard like he's the only bird there. Tom doesn't let anybody put him in a corner.

The person that hands your coffee out the window at Starbucks in the morning might not be in their forever job, but that warm cup of coffee sure makes you feel great, doesn't it? The highway worker outside in the pouring rain is shivering as he directs you safely into a clear path away from the road construction, but he's out there providing a service that makes the world a safer place. Hopefully, they're getting paid enough for their time and aren't suffering through their days. If you are in a job, situation, or relationship that requires you to suffer through your days, you are making a choice to be in that place, and you are the only one responsible for keeping yourself in that spot. Up your game if you want to get into a different job. What percentage are you putting out into the world? Are you doing your best? Are you shining where you've been planted?

- Are there areas in your life where you feel as though you are suffering?

- What changes could you make to improve those areas?

- Are you ready to be done suffering?

Chapter 14

Success Isn't about Luck—Write Your Map

Adopt the pace of nature: her secret is patience.

—Ralph Waldo Emerson

A great life is not about luck. It is not something that mysteriously happens while you are lying on the couch at home, trying to decide whether to call out sick from work. Working with clients for thirty-five plus years has given me a bit of a window into the lives of people, and there are some obvious common denominators in those people who have obtained success.

Successful people are doers; they aren't the ones sitting around waiting for the perfect opportunity to fall out of the sky. They create their own opportunities. They've learned that no doesn't always mean no; sometimes, it means try harder, work harder, or find a different way. These people have discovered that sometimes, it's better to lead and that you don't get ahead by just following the pack. I love my sheep, but I don't see much when I look into their eyes. They follow each other around baaing with no real idea where the leader of the herd is taking them, and the reality is they don't much care. They are sweet and gentle, but they are herd animals. They go wherever the herd is being led. The most successful clients are not the ones following the herd.

Some clients have different careers or jobs every time we meet. They are like serial killers, but what they keep killing is every job or business they touch. The boss was a dick, or the market just wasn't ready for their great idea. Some clients constantly call with one great idea after another but can't ever seem to get any of them off the ground. They flit from thing to thing and get bored with their amazing ideas sometimes before they've even launched them. Most businesses take years to develop, and relationships with clients are hard-won and require patience to build. If you want to get ahead in your job, give one hundred and provide some results before asking for that next raise. If you are building a business, try putting out some dogged determinedness and deliver consistently good services or products.

The E-Myth by Michael Gerber is a must-read for anyone looking to be successful in business. This book illustrates the importance of developing systems that make every business operate in the same ways that larger businesses operate. Small business owners start a business with a great idea but don't usually see the need or necessity for systems. Businesses are often started without having a solid foundation under them. The owners fail to understand the importance of delivering consistently good products with every sale or service. Small businesses often lack consistency. There are no systems in place to support the business when issues arise or needs must be addressed. Any business, large or small, operates based on a set of systems. Failure to establish these systems is one of the main reasons for a business's demise. Consistency is key for the survival of any business, large or small.

People that don't have great jobs or businesses love to comment about how lucky the people are that have these things. Pointing out how lucky successful people are is simply an excuse for someone who can't get their own act together. It also diminishes the hard work that another person has put into building something. I've spent years building a successful business, and nothing pisses me off more than someone who minimizes my efforts as just lucky. Luck didn't build my business. Luck didn't get out of bed every day, put a smile on its face, and meet with my clients. Tenacity, consistency, doggedness, long hours, patience, continued education, and persistence are the skills needed to build a business or succeed in a career. The people I see climbing ladders to success are the ones putting in the hours and pushing hard when everyone else has already left for the day. Success isn't about luck. It's not an event or a destination. It's a journey.

In my career, I've had a few clients that hit large lottery winnings. One client won fifteen million, and the other won ten million. The fun thing is that they both won the same year within months of each other, and both called me from lottery headquarters when they were trying to decide whether to take their winnings in a lump sum or in equal payments. These people got lucky.

> Mike was down on his luck when I met him. He was going through a bitter divorce, and he was buried in debt. He even cried during our first meeting. He felt like he had fallen so far down in the past couple of years. He was broken, sad, and lonely. I told him a story that I tell many clients. "Don't worry," I told him, "this is the conversation we are having today. Next year, your story will be different. In five years, it will be entirely different, and I will remind you of how far you've come." He smiled and said that he hoped things would start turning around soon. About nine months later, I received a phone call from lottery headquarters. Mike had two things to tell me. He was newly married, and he had just won fifteen million dollars. He said he wasn't going to have to wait five years for things to come around.

Most clients don't get that kind of luck, and the ones that get ahead work hard for it. They spend years working on building healthy relationships, businesses, and careers. Their lives aren't always pretty and glamorous; sometimes, they are downright messy. Knowing clients over a period of many years means seeing them weather periods of highs and periods of lows. The best among them will endure the struggles and tragedies, and the ones that do the work will consistently rise above the people not willing to put in the time.

A successful career and life require careful planning and huge amounts of tenacity.

The first step is to design the life of your dreams. Visualize this life you want to live. See it, feel it, smell it, taste it! What does this dream look like? What things define success for you? Success means different things to different people. Create a vision of your success. Can you see yourself living this life? Moving through your days in a contented haze of success. Our brains are machines that work even when we are not consciously aware of it. If you don't develop a clear picture of what success means to you, then your brain, the most powerful tool in your toolbox, has nothing to work toward. Did you know that we only consciously use ten percent of our brain's capacity and that the other ninety percent is working on our dreams behind the scenes without our awareness? That's why you need to give your brain a design and a vision. Post images and pictures on your refrigerator or the walls in your office. The remarkable thing is that even when you are not consciously thinking about these things, your brain, the brilliant computer in your head, will continue to work on them. While you are sleeping, eating, having sex, working, walking, and exercising, you are using ten percent of your brain. The other ninety percent is working on your dream of the life you want to live without you being aware of it. That's like having ninety people out there plowing your fields and planting your crops while you're hanging out with ten friends at the movies!

Once you've developed your dream and vision, work on a map. You know what you want, so now how are you going to get there? Identify goals and landmarks that will mark your success along the path.

Make three lists:

- Short-term goals: less than one year

- Long-term goals: one to five years

- Lifetime goals: identify when you plan to reach these goals.

Rewards: List out rewards that you get at each milestone. If your lifetime goal is retirement, the reward will be owning your own time.

These goals are not negotiable, so for them to work, you need to use terms that don't leave room for compromise. A one-year goal of paying off your credit card debt would read "eliminate credit card debt in six months," not "I hope or want to eliminate credit card debt." Making your goals flexible means that you have room to negotiate them. Your goals need to be realistic, and you need to have a plan for how you will accomplish them. If the goal is to pay off a credit card debt of six thousand dollars within six months, identify where you will find this money. For example, reduce spending on clothing and dining out for six months to eliminate six thousand in credit card debt. Next, work on the mechanics. Make a credit card payment of one thousand dollars each month until the debt is eliminated. Once the debt is eliminated, you can follow that goal up with one that requires you to pay your credit card debt off in full each month.

Steps like these are demanding work, but they will get you to the life you dream of living. The things we work for that come with a price bring with them the pride of accomplishment. Work hard; get the prize. If your only plan is to wait until you win millions in the lottery, the odds are good that you will be waiting for an exceptionally long time.

- What does your dream life look like?

- Can you visualize this life of your dreams?

- What does the map you need to get to that life entail?

- Develop your goals. Short-term, long-term, and lifetime.

- How will you get to these goals?

- What rewards do you want as you reach your goals?

Chapter 15
Stop Doubting

> A garden is a grand teacher. It teaches patience and careful watchfulness; it teaches industry and thrift; above all, it teaches entire trust.
>
> —Gertrude Jekyll

> You gain strength, courage, and confidence by every experience in which you really stop to look fear in the face. You are able to say to yourself, "I lived through this horror. I can take the next thing that comes along." You must do the thing you think you cannot do.
>
> —Eleanor Roosevelt

Do you think a farmer stops to question whether his seeds will grow? Have you ever planted tomato plants? The seeds are so tiny that I use a pencil eraser to pick them up and place them into the soil. By the end of the summer, these plants will climb to be eight or ten feet tall. Farmers and gardeners can't question whether the seeds they plant will grow. They prepare the soil, wait for the right weather, and plant their seeds. Sometimes, the weather won't cooperate, and crops will be lost, but we will all plant again. Life requires that we cast aside our doubts and try again the next season. Without the hope and optimism that our tiny seeds will grow to produce an amazing crop, what do we have? When we let doubt sour our efforts or when we are too jaded to even attempt to grow our crops, all is lost.

Doubt and fear are lousy bed partners that creep under my bedroom door at night and slink into my warm bed. I often lay there, tossing and turning while they wreak their havoc on my mind. They find the holes in all my best-laid plans and lament on and on about the failures sure to follow. They are horrible to sleep with, but in the morning light, they slither away again. They are small and powerless in the light of day, and the stories of failures they whispered in my ear all night long seem weak and feeble. They have stolen my sleep, and I am happy to see them disappear.

Do you have nights or days like that? There are so many nights I have spent with my mind spinning and hashing doomsday plans, only to wake up in the morning and see how foolish all my doubts and fears were. Sometimes, the doubts and fears I have are reminiscent of the voices of different people that have crossed through my life. "You can't do that!" "You can't have that!" "Nobody does those things!" It has taken me years to oust these negative voices from my head, and in moments of change or weakness, they still try to work their way back in. When they manage to sneak in, I work hard to kick their asses out the door as soon as possible.

> Kathy has been a client for thirty-five years. She's been in a miserable marriage for thirty-nine years, and it's been painful to watch. At one appointment, she was missing a few teeth. Other years, she has worn the bruises her husband gave her, like a pair of earrings or a string of pearls. They are decorations on her wounded soul. "Kevin's been having a rough year," she said. "He's only drinking so much because he's depressed." One time when she threatened to leave him, he drove their car into the other lane of traffic toward oncoming cars with their four kids in the back of the car, screaming at her until she agreed to stay. She called me another time, sobbing because she had just found out she was pregnant with their fifth child. "How will we afford another child?" she

asked. She was the main breadwinner, and he was a self-employed builder. He refused to pay taxes and had amassed over a hundred thousand dollars in tax debt. "Can't you get the IRS to put him in jail?" she would ask. One time, a neighbor called social services when she found Kevin attempting to smother the new baby under a couch cushion. "I have to go to work," she said, "and someone has to watch the kids." In the beginning, I tried to help. I shared books and the name of a friend who worked at a shelter for abused women. Every year, we discussed her situation, but she had too many fears and doubts about her ability to live on her own. "I'm not strong like you," she would say. "My mother and father are both alcoholics, and they are still married. I'm a Catholic, and we don't divorce." Her children are all grown now, and they show all the signs of the situation they were raised in. Kathy and her husband are still married, but she has a longtime boyfriend that she keeps on the side. Every time we meet, she says that someday she will finally leave him. I know better though. Death will part them before she finally finds the courage to leave.

You can lead a horse to the water, but sometimes, you can't make him get in the trailer. In 2013, my daughter, Meg, reached out to her photographer friend, Katie. Her horse, Brownie, was getting on in age, and she wanted to get some pictures of him at the beach before it was too late. They picked a day to meet at the beach. There was a northeaster coming in later that night, so the light was fabulous, and the surf was up. The conditions looked promising for a fabulous photo shoot. Brownie walked onto the trailer, and they headed for the beach. They got a ton of incredible shots with Meg and Brownie in the surf looking out at the incoming waves, and the framed photos still hang on my walls. Brownie's ears are forward in his normal inquisitive state, and he is in his element, frolicking in the sand and surf. The resulting photos were amazing. At dusk, they decided to load up and head home, but Brownie refused to walk back into the trailer. In fact, he spent the next five hours refusing to walk on the trailer. Multiple family members and friends went to the beach to help Meg, but every time they approached the trailer, he dug in all his eleven hundred pounds and refused to load. The surf was getting heavier, the night was getting darker, and they were still no closer to getting Brownie on the trailer. Finally, Meg played her final card. She made a call to her friend, Katelyn, who coached her on the equestrian team in college. They had become quite a team at showing and loading difficult horses. She hated to get her out of bed so late at night, but desperation had set in. Katelyn lived half an hour away, and sure enough, half an hour after the call, everyone at the beach heard Katelyn's big diesel truck making its way toward the beach parking lot. Brownie's ears pricked forward when he heard the distinctive rumble of the truck and, without further ado, trotted onto the trailer just as Katelyn's headlights swung into view. The point is that sometimes, it doesn't matter how much effort you put into trying to help people move in a better direction. They get the message and make the move when they're ready to hear the message.

> Julie was having difficulty reentering the workforce after staying home to raise her children. She had spent the last five years debating about what job she should try. We all offered suggestions, but she found a reason why they were all wrong. Finally, she decided to try tax preparation. "It's been a lucky career for you," she said, "so I think I'll give it a try." She signed up for a three-month tax class and soon was working for a national tax preparation chain, making minimum wage. Within a short time, she was working sixty to seventy hours per week. She was stressed and miserable and felt like she was never home. When she developed an itchy rash all over her body, she called to com-

plain about what a horrible choice she had made. "This is a miserable job," she said, so when the tax season ended, she took a real estate class. A few months later, she was complaining that there was no money to be made in real estate at that time, so she accepted another entry-level, low-paying job at a department store. Once again, she was working crazy hours for minimum wage, grumbling about the lack of good job opportunities in her area and scratching at her itchy stress-induced rash. She whined that everyone else had a great job and was making tons of money.

Most of us limit ourselves and put ceilings on what we can accomplish. Clients often come in with a list of complaints but don't really want solutions. For some, complaining is a lifelong habit they are so enmeshed in that they can't imagine there's a better way. There are people I know that will find fault with every opportunity that presents itself. Offer them some easy solutions, and they are quick to shoot down everything offered with a reason why it won't work for them. Their answers are always similar enough to be memorized. That won't work for me. That doesn't work in this part of the country. I'm too old to try that. I'm not smart enough, strong enough, or educated enough. For some people, misery is an addiction they are not willing to give up. The doubts and fears in their own mind are ones they aren't ready to evict. Time and experience have been great teachers in helping me move on from trying to help these people. Some of them are simply more comfortable staying where they are than trying to get out of a bad situation.

- What doubts or fears do you have?

- How do they impact your ability to own your greatest life?

- What truths can you tell yourself to eliminate these doubts or fears?

Chapter 16
The Reality of Karma

Fuck with it, and karma will bite you in the ass.

—Sherri Mahoney

Call it by any name you like; karma is the great equalizer. Do you want great results in life? Put forth great effort. Treat people how you want to be treated. When faced with the choice to do the right thing, always take the high road. Karma has a way of rewarding people who honor that path. Recently, I read a Facebook post a woman had written asking how to get back at a person who had hurt someone close to her. I was pleased to see that most of the responses told her to just wait. You see, karma has a way of balancing things out. Do you doubt this?

> Chris was a self-employed truck driver who became a client a few years after recovering from surgery to remove a brain tumor. His girlfriend was helping him get his life together and had directed him toward me. He hadn't filed taxes in five or six years, so with the help of his girlfriend, I prepared the returns and got him back on track. A few years after I met him, Chris won a million dollars on a scratch ticket. He hooked up with a legal firm in Boston that advised him to put all the money into a trust with him as a benefi-

ciary. At the time, it seemed like they were just creating an unnecessary expense for him. Chris started telling people that he hadn't been the one to scratch the ticket, but I clearly remembered him telling me that it was his. I wondered about the discrepancy. Each year, I would get documents from his legal team and would file his tax return reporting the earnings from his winnings. The trust would pay any tax liability. Five years or so after the lottery win, I received a subpoena. It seems my client, Chris, forgot to tell me that he'd been dodging child support for years. His daughter has some special needs, and her mother, his ex-girlfriend, was struggling. She'd been supporting everything on her own for a few years but, much to Chris' dismay, had found out about his lottery winnings. At the hearing, I was called to testify that the return being presented to the court was the one that I prepared on Chris's behalf. The judge asked me to look at the return. It was definitely one that my firm printed and provided to the client, but something was wrong. On page two of the return, someone had crossed out the total income printed on the return, and an amount handwritten with a Sharpie marker had been scrawled on the line. There were a few other spots where dollar amounts had been crossed out and new amounts were written in. It looked like a child had scribbled numbers on the page, and the amounts didn't even total properly. Clearly, the income on the return was altered, and the judge was not pleased that someone tampered with the return. He was not merciful in his ruling, and Chris lost a large chunk of winnings toward the support of his daughter. The judge also required Chris to take out a large life

> insurance policy with his daughter as beneficiary and have a will drafted with her as beneficiary as well. He filed an appeal but developed another brain tumor before his appeal could be heard and passed away a year later. Lady Karma had proven herself to be even less merciful than the judge that ruled against him.

The energy we put out attracts a like-kind reaction. Be generous with your time, money, and resources, and these things will flow in your direction with ease. When you approach a situation with a nasty tone or a demeaning attitude, the response you receive is likely to mirror your own. A smile disarms even the trickiest situation and is most often returned in kind. Try making a smile the first part of your wardrobe you put on every morning. As I write this, the year 2021 is ending, and we are all masked again. It's not possible to see whether we are being greeted with a smile, and I have noticed that people look toward my eyes for the conveyance of a smile. We are all smiling with our eyes now! A smile is the easiest way to initiate positive communication, and when we can't see each other's lips, our eyes are the next best indicator. Look in the mirror at how your eyes change when you smile.

> There is a fellow, Peter, who I hire to paint and hang wallpaper for me. Peter's positive energy is contagious, and he always points out the beauty in the day or how beautiful the view out the window is. He is in high demand and has a regular following of people, all waiting for him to come and work his magic in their homes. He tells me that he likes his simple life, and he fills his home with dozens of beautiful plants. He has two kids and is grateful for his ex-spouse's husband, who works at a great college that has allowed his boys to get an amazing education at no cost. He exudes a karma that invites good things into his life.

The actions we put forth into the world invite a response, and the energy we exude can invite either a positive or negative response. I've met and had conversations with people with such amazing energy that their positive vibe resonates in the room long after they've departed. On the other hand, I've met other people whose energy was so negative that I couldn't wait for them to leave. Sometimes, after an especially bitter client has gone, I've left the outside door open or opened my window just to feel some cleansing air. Toxic energy can cling to a client's paperwork long after they've left the room.

> Phil was a man of smoke and mirrors. A leader in town politics and well-liked by most people, he came to me when he made the decision to sell his business. I was surprised when he told me he hadn't filed tax returns in five years. His voice took on a nasty tone when he talked about his wife and the problems in his life. A former employee of his cautioned me about him. He had slapped her and shoved her when she didn't move fast enough for him. Other people had similar stories of mistreatment at his hands. He sold his business for less than he thought it was worth and soon butted heads with the new owner, who he had promised to train. He was angry when the new owner successfully grew the business into a profitable venture, and he quickly spent the money he had made on the sale of the business. The passing years and his lack of money made him even more bitter, and eventually, his wife divorced him. She needed some happiness in her life, and his anger with the world was pushing him further away. He worked a series of jobs that all made him miserable until he sadly took his own life before his sixty-fifth birthday.

The view across my desk has shown me that success and prosperity come easier to those with good karma. Too often, the people that seem to be struggling year after year are those who exude an aura of negative energy. They are the ones bickering with their neighbors or fighting with their children and parents. On the other hand, the ones that bring in a smile and kind words often have stories of success and happiness. For me, the connection has been easily identifiable.

The great news is that we can decide to change the energy we are putting into the world. Try being kind to the person serving your dinner or handing your coffee out the window. Smile at your cashier or the person bagging your groceries. Small gestures of kindness invite good karma into our lives. Do the right thing even when it's difficult. Go the extra mile to lighten someone else's load. Open your heart and be there for a friend or family member in need. Support the people in your life financially to the extent you can afford. Be fair and be just. A clenched fist is not open to receive the gifts life is dropping toward your palm. Open your mind, your heart, and your mouth in the ways of kindness. You can decide what energy to spread as you move throughout your day. Make conscious choices that support positivity, and Lady Karma will smile your way.

- Do you recognize the connection between the energy you put forth and the results you get?

- Can you remember times when you felt like karma had gone against you?

- Do you feel like you get better results when you exude a certain kind of energy?

- Can you identify people in your life that have had positive energy?

Chapter 17

The Money Will Follow—Money Really Does Grow on Trees

> The best time to plant a tree was twenty years ago. The second-best time is now.
>
> —Chinese Proverb

A tiny seed planted in fertile soil can produce a large tree, and likewise, ideas of financial success, when planted into fertile minds, can also grow to produce amazingly successful financial lives. Growing up a child in the seventies, I heard oft-repeated idioms such as *money doesn't grow on trees* and *waste not want not*. Then there's my all-time, most-hated phrase, "What, do you think we are made of money?" Funny, in my business, I have met so many people hiding their financial disasters behind a carefully constructed curtain of smoke and mirrors. People will openly talk about their sex lives, their difficulties getting pregnant, and a multitude of other things, but most people are loathed to discuss their financial problems. Why is money or financial failure such a shameful topic?

> Recently, I attempted to negotiate the purchase of a cabin that had been in my family for many years. My intent was to keep this property in the family for my children and grandchildren to enjoy. Amid negotiations, the seller (a family member)

lamented his hatred of money. Right then, I knew that the potential sale was doomed to failure. Sure enough, the asking price ended up being driven by his knowledge of my desire to purchase the property, what he thought I could pay, and not representative of the actual cost he had paid or the current value. As much as I would have liked to purchase the property, I was not willing to overpay and be victimized by someone who had such negative energy around money.

Money has energy attached to it. You can attract money to you by connecting positive energy to money in your life, or you can push it away by attaching a negative value to it. Money itself is not a precursor for happiness. Some of the saddest people I know have vast amounts of money. Money can make your life easier, but it will never be a guarantee of happiness. Money will not buy you happiness, but it will give you choices, freedom, and options to make decisions about how you spend your days. For this reason, the pursuit of money is worth the chase.

I've spent my career studying the habits and emotions people have surrounding their money. It's a topic I love to explore, and the relationship that people have with money has always fascinated me. I have collaborated with clients from all walks of life: there are clients with huge homes and bank accounts who are too miserable to get out of bed in the morning, and then there are others with very little who always find happiness in their days. I've easily dismissed money as a source of happiness, although I do know that for many, the struggle to live with little money can often make life more difficult.

Most people are looking for more money, and some will find it while others will not. My curiosity has compelled me to study both the habits of those who have found a way to grow money, as well as the habits of others who can't seem to get their seeds to germinate. I've observed some common traits in the people who attract wealth, and these tend to be missing in those who don't. Money, I've discovered, really does grow on trees. Let me share with you now the secrets to growing wealth.

To grow money, you need good seeds. Are the seeds of your ideas fresh and relevant, or are they old and leftover from falsehoods passed down through generational dysfunction? If your seeds are old, you will need to replace them with new, fresh seeds. Old decaying seeds will not germinate. Let go of beliefs that don't serve you. They will not aid you in your financial growth.

Additionally, the soil that receives the seeds you are planting needs to be fertile and fresh. Fertilize the soil of your mind with freshly composted and aerated thoughts. Make room in the soil of your mind for innovative ideas. Your ideas will need room to germinate.

- Give your money tree the support it needs. It's okay to get outside help with this. Sometimes, you need an expert to show you the path to growth. Consult with a therapist or coach. Mend your broken bits.

- Amend your soil and rid it of weeds. If you have negative weeds or thoughts in your soil, your healthy seedlings will be suffocated and will not be able to thrive.

- Eliminate toxicity from your soil, for it will poison your healthy seedlings. Your seedlings need every bit of support you can give them, and the soil of your mind needs to be free of emotional poisons that do not support your great financial dreams. Surround yourself with people that support your success.

- Control the elements that affect the visions of your financial seedlings' growth to the largest extent possible. Don't waste your efforts planting your ideas on hostile ground. Remove negativity from your life as much as possible.

- Provide fertilizer for your money tree as it grows. Plant it in areas that provide adequate amounts of light and rain. Make sure your environment supports the tree you want to grow. Water your ideas with healthy nutrients when necessary. Feed your dreams!

- Soil that is barren or rock hard will not provide a hospitable foundation to receive your seedlings. When the timing and elements are right, money will flow easily. Don't force it. If the elements are right, they will grow. Follow opportunities but move on if things don't flow naturally.

- Accept the money tree for what it is. The purpose of your money tree is to provide you with freedom and options. It will never fix all your problems or guarantee you a wonderful life. Bring balance and happiness to other areas of your life so that when money flows your way, you can fully enjoy it.

- Know that moving your money tree to a new location will not solve any problems if you don't fix the soil, pull the weeds, and fertilize the tree. You need to fix the problems at the roots of your tree, not in the topmost branches.

- Don't expect luck to grow your money tree. Plan to invest hard work and be prepared to pay attention to every detail. Watch for pests and critters looking to undermine the growth of your tree. Work hard to reap the rewards of a great financial harvest.

- Develop a plan and goals for the growth of your money tree. Your tree will have diverse needs as it grows. You will need to rewrite your plan so that you can address the growth of your money tree. When the path you are following is no longer productive, look for other opportunities. Failures don't make us a failure; they teach us what we need to know in order to succeed in the next season.

- Feel the connection between your body and your money tree. Experience the connection between the growth and health of your tree and your body's health. As your tree grows, enjoy its shade and the fruit it produces. Its growth will nourish you. It will bend its limbs to provide you shelter. Don't deny yourself the pleasure of experiencing the bounty your tree has to offer.

- Have faith that given the proper soil, nutrients, fertilizer, and elements, your money tree will grow. Push away your doubts and fears. Do not let your doubts and fears inhibit your growth plans. Plant seeds for success even when you are afraid or have doubts about your success.

- Experience the happiness of watching your money tree grow. Smile upon your tree every day and watch it grow. Attend to your tree, admire your tree, and marvel at its growth. Push joy toward your tree and watch it jump toward the sky in response!

- Practice positive karma by encouraging the growth of other people's money trees. Offer to help them grow their trees when given the opportunity. Don't step on or condemn other people's plans or trees. They don't all have to look like yours. Water each other's trees with shared ideas for growth.

Today is a great day to start a money tree, and in the following chapter, I will share a few seeds to help you grow your tree. Tiny seeds can grow huge financial success. The soil of your mind is fertile and ready to grow the financial success of your dreams! Let's grow your money tree!

Chapter 18

Good Habits Breed Success

Success doesn't come from what you do occasionally.
It comes from what you do consistently.

—Marie Forleo

Gardens are not made by singing "Oh, how
beautiful," and sitting in the shade.

—Rudyard Kipling

People do not decide their futures. They decide their
habits, and their habits decide their futures.

—F. M. Alexander

The little habits you perform every day are ritualistic, and they can either set you up for success or else wash away all the tiny seeds you're attempting to grow. Isn't it ironic that it seems like the people with the least amount of money are the ones stopping every day for cigarettes, lottery tickets, and booze on their way by their local convenience store? These terrible habits that feed unhealthy addictions are bound to keep these people locked into a long journey of poverty.

Alternatively, there are habits you can establish that will direct you down a path of success. Certain habits encourage success while others produce negative results. A behavior repeated for an average of sixty-six days becomes automatic. The choice of which behaviors to adopt is yours. You can decide to create healthy habits that propel you forward or negative habits that keep you down.

Habits, once established, are difficult to change, but replacing negative habits with positive habits is a crucial step in your path to success.

The Morning Miracle by Hal Elrod is a short, amazing book worth reading multiple times. A common trait among successful people is their morning routine. Establishing a routine that supports you during the day lays the foundation to make every day a success. Invest sixty-six days in developing a series of positive habits in the morning and see how your life changes. I developed my own morning routine many years ago, and it supports me as I accomplish the goals I've set for each day and helps ensure my success. To have a wonderful day, it's important to get both my head and my body in alignment, and morning habits that include meditation, affirmations, visualization, and yoga accomplish those goals for me. Getting out of bed early gives me the time needed to do these things, and this time in the morning is one of the best gifts I can give myself. These habits have become so ingrained in my life that they require no thought to implement. Time has taught me to be kind to myself when the habits I have planned for the morning get derailed, but most mornings my routine goes something like this:

- Morning alarm goes off at 5:00 a.m.

- Drink a glass of ice water with lemon, followed by apple cider vinegar tea for digestion. A highlight of my morning is a tea made with two teaspoons of Bragg Miracle Cleanse with boiling water. If I can't get the Bragg Miracle Cleanse, I make my own with two teaspoons of Bragg Apple Cider Vinegar, one teaspoon of honey, a dash of cayenne pepper, and a squeeze of lemon. This concoction tastes fabulous, is addictive, and provides strong support for intestinal health and maintaining weight. I've been drinking this vinegar tea for over twenty years and have never had to take an antacid or other medication for stomach problems.

- Meditate for ten minutes. Meditation does not come easily to me, but I've learned to master it (usually). Deep breathing helps, along with consciously sweeping thoughts out of my head as they arise. The clarity I get from meditation is necessary for keeping me organized during the day. If you've got misgivings about meditation, now is the time to kick them to the curb. Most people I know who meditate aren't doing it in a room full of people in the lotus position, chanting "ohm." There are loggers, builders, and people from all walks of life who meditate. Meditation is the reboot my brain needs in the morning to clean out the junk files that clutter my head. I want my days to be productive, my thoughts uncontaminated, and meditation clears out the roadblocks. I practice meditation first thing in the morning while I wait for my tea water to boil. It's a deep cleaning my brain needs before I start loading it up with all the day's tasks.

- Affirmations (five minutes)—I use affirmations to direct my focus toward whatever I am currently working on. If I'm having anxiety about the upcoming tax season, I focus my affirmations on being stress-free. Prior to writing this book, I developed "the information you need is in your head and it's time to write the book" affirmation. My morning affirmations focus positive thoughts toward areas where I'm having stress or need encouragement. Repeating an affirmation helps give your mind direction and quells fears and doubts you might be having about specific issues. Affirmations convince your mind that you can accomplish your goals. Repeating an affirmation on a regular basis makes success in obtaining your goals the only acceptable path.

- Visualization (five minutes)—visualizing something you are working toward or stressing about gives your brain a positive vision to follow. If I'm stressing about an upcoming tax season, I will visualize myself flowing through the season calmly and without stress. Before writing this book, I envisioned myself sitting in a serene place as I sat typing and reflecting, surrounded by pine trees with snow softly falling. Developing the vision provides the visual map that you want your brain to follow. Events may cross through your day to disrupt your energy, but pulling that visualization back into focus reminds your brain to hold onto your vision for the day. Visualizing the reality you hope to obtain arms your brain with the vision for your success. This vision makes the dream an achievable goal because your mind has already seen it. I often feel a sense of déjà vu when I accomplish goals because I have already seen these goals come to fruition in my mind's eye.

- Yoga (thirty minutes)—yoga has been my exercise of choice for over thirty years, and I usually include strength training or cardio. I especially like the Beachbody Piyo or P90 series of workouts. Sitting for extended periods of time with my shoulders hunched, reaching toward a keyboard bothers my hips and shoulders, so I've discovered exercises that open my shoulders and build leg strength. Many years ago, I had severe back pain that finally brought me to a chiropractor. An article I read promoted yoga for back health, and I've been doing daily yoga and avoiding back pain ever since. As we age, it's important to maintain our flexibility, and morning yoga loosens the muscles and warms up our joints. Not only does yoga loosen my joints, but I also often find that my best ideas flow into my head when I'm doing yoga in the morning. Focusing on my breathing and stretching my limbs leaves my brain open for the flow of ideas.

- My typical go-to breakfast of choice is a morning smoothie made in a NutriBullet. I drink this while exercising and take it to the office in the morning. The recipe varies but usually includes a combination of the following: organic coconut milk, organic spinach, blueberries, protein powder, half a banana, one quarter of an avocado, almond butter, and ice. I don't think it matters what you eat for breakfast, but it's important that whatever you eat is healthy so that it fuels your body and your mind. The right food keeps your mind sharp and helps to eliminate brain fog.

You can implement some or all these habits or add a few of your own. The important thing is to establish a healthy morning routine that will support your body and steer you toward a successful day. It's all about giving yourself the tools to get your head and body in a place that will allow you to operate at the highest level possible. Be gentle with yourself when life interferes with your morning plans. Sometimes if I've had a late or sleepless night, 5:00 a.m. is simply too early to get up, or early client meetings require that my affirmations happen in my morning shower. Sometimes my brain simply won't slow down enough for me to meditate. The important thing is that most mornings follow the routine of the healthy habits you develop.

In the meantime, perhaps these fresh, healthy habits will replace some stale, harmful habits you might have. Once firmly rooted, these new behaviors will bring you some amazing satisfaction!

An interesting thing about habits is that creating beneficial habits in one area will flow into other areas of your life. We often have groups of habits that we do around different phases of our day; this methodology is called habit stacking. Most of us have groups of habits centered around our morning routine, exercise routine, work routine, food preparation routine, and shopping routines. We do these things so automatically that we can miss the opportunity to improve our routines because these systems we've designed are so ingrained. Sometimes, we need to examine our methodology and ask ourselves if there could potentially be a better way of doing something.

Many years ago, amid a troubled marriage, a friend pointed out something obvious to her but about which I was completely in the dark. "You know," she said, "it's amazing how clean and beautiful your house is, but your closets are a total disaster." That required some deep thinking on my part. Her observation was particularly insightful, and it was the impetus I needed to explore the situation. I had a beautiful, well-kept home, but my closets were stuffed from floor to ceiling with piles of crap that made it difficult to even close the doors. These closets were symbolic of the life I was living. The man I was married to was a controlling, alcoholic narcissist, and it took all my energy to maintain his moods and the facade of my perfect life. Every ounce of energy I had went into maintaining that image, and I stuffed everything else away. Eventually, my need to be a good parent to our two daughters took precedence over my need to maintain this man, and I suffered through the bitter divorce to get to the light on the other side. Our habits can reveal quite a bit if we are willing to examine them.

Our habits can be as simple as the way we get out of bed in the morning, brush our teeth, and shower, but they also play a part in how we manage our relationships with money. Clients betray their habits with money in tiny pieces of information they exchange during our relationship.

> Sheila was a writer. She hadn't filed tax returns in five years, and she was getting tax notices from the IRS. She dropped off boxes full of documents for us to go through to obtain the yearly income, expense amounts, and forms necessary to prepare her tax returns. In the process of going through her boxes, we found quite a bit beside the necessary tax documents. Along with the expected piles of bills and tax notices, we found royalty checks (uncashed), dividend checks (also uncashed), checks from an inheritance (again, uncashed), love letters from multiple lovers, and letters from her mother with whom she was feud-

ing. She asked that we read everything and put together piles of documents with notes suggesting the required action. We weren't quite sure what to tell her regarding her relationship with her mother.

Clients are often financial wrecks with piles of disorganized paperwork, multiple bank accounts, and investment accounts floating around. They file their tax returns late, have their insurances canceled, cell phones shut off, and end up borrowing money to keep their heads above water. I once told a client that over the years, he had spent more money paying me to clean up his tax disasters than he would have if he had just filed the returns on time and paid the damn taxes. Bad money habits will end up costing you more in the long run.

It's not a stretch to suggest that developing healthy habits with money will allow money to flow into your life more easily. Do you want more money in your life? Court it like a lover you'd like to get into your bed. Study it, pursue it, and shower it with attention. It only makes sense that better habits about money will bring more of it into your life.

Start small with manageable goals for your morning routine. As your life changes, implement other healthy routines in your work environment and develop habits that support your financial goals. Give your new beneficial habits time to develop their roots. You can only grow upward from here.

- What habits can you implement that will support you in the morning?

- Examine your current daily routines. Are they serving you or working against you?

- Are there better habits or systems you can implement to support you in your work?

- Do you have good habits surrounding your money?

- What habits could you learn to support your financial growth?

Chapter 19
Financial Lessons—Little Baskets

The price of anything is the amount of life you exchange for it.

—Henry David Thoreau

Two roads diverged in a wood, and I took the one less traveled by, and that has made all the difference.

—Robert Frost

We are all in the exchange business, exchanging bits of our time for money. Unfortunately, most of us will enter adulthood with few skills in money management. To meet our financial goals, we will need to develop a clear vision of what we want our future to look like and a map to direct us on how to get there.

Reaching our financial goals will require self-discipline since we will need to make decisions about how to fund and pay for the things we need and want in our life. Storing all your money in only one basket without directing resources toward other baskets for savings or large purchases will leave you scrambling when you hit retirement age or at the mercy of lenders when you want to make large purchases. Directing money into different baskets will help you meet diverse needs as they arise. What baskets are you currently funding? The following are examples of baskets you might need to fund:

- Living Expenses

- Retirement
- College Savings
- Large Purchases
- Vacation Fund
- Charitable Giving
- Emergency Fund

Most of us work the typical five days on, two days off schedule. We exchange our time, usually forty hours per week, for a certain salary or hourly rate. Some people work the sixth and even seventh day as well to increase their earnings. The typical retirement funding plan is often ten percent or less of a person's wages. Whether that amount is enough to ensure a comfortable retirement depends on the exchange rate for the time worked. In other words, if the salary or hourly rate is insufficient to not only fund the basket for living expenses but also to allow the other baskets to be funded, you will find yourself lacking when it comes time to pay for colleges, large repairs, vacations, or retirement.

We've been taught to subsidize the things we want or think we need through the accumulation of debt. We fund a college education with student loans, purchases such as cars and boats with personal loans, and pay for vacations and other large ticket items with credit cards. Of course, this debt then requires the additional expense of interest, which is the cost of using someone else's money. A meager retirement fund, coupled with a ton of debt, will often leave a person with barely enough money to cover basic expenses. To top it off, a hiccup in employment, a medical issue, or any other reason that causes difficulty meeting expenses will often force people to tap into their retirement accounts early, further reducing the funds available when they retire. For many, it's a long journey of hard work culminating in the realization that they aren't going to be able to enjoy the things they've looked forward to for years. That's hardly a great return for forty years of servitude.

Do you believe there could be a better way? I do, and one of the driving forces behind me wanting to share this book with you was to tell you that you can follow a different path. I dreamed of a different path for myself, and I have helped hundreds and hundreds of clients change the course of their paths. If you are willing to slice through the fog and step forward through the noise of what everyone else is doing or everything you've been told to do, you will see that there is another path. It may not be as clearly marked because it is less traveled, but it is there if you are willing to pursue it.

Follow this less-traveled path. You don't have to stay on the same path that everyone else is on. Resist the urge to stay stuck in the bottom of the crab pot and begin the climb to the top. Write your own map. There are many books and articles worth reading that can help you make healthy financial changes in your life, but not everything you read or learn will be the right fit for you. I've read many books by proclaimed experts in offering financial guidance, and I've learned a little from each of them. What I've found, though, is that part of my own journey was discovering what pieces of information worked best for me.

When my husband and I were younger, we read a series of books by a well-known self-help author that suggested his readers acquire rental properties. We took all the prescribed steps, followed his outlined plan, and liquidated some of the equity in our home to acquire two apartment buildings with a total of six apartments. At the onset, we were excited and willing to work hard to rehabilitate these apartments and provide beautiful living spaces for our tenants. We made the mistake of not understanding the social economics of the neighborhoods our buildings were in and quickly discovered that our tenants didn't care about beautiful apartments. Most of them just didn't want to pay rent, and tenants would do just about anything to avoid doing so. One tenant would smash a broom handle into a vintage glass, kitchen cabinet doors and then call the board of health to complain about the broken glass every time we attempted to collect rent. Others would squat in their apartment, turn off the lights, and hide whenever we went to collect their rent. One year, my husband was in housing court weekly, trying to evict an old woman fronting for a bunch of drug-dealing grandkids. Every time she showed up for court, she would wheel in her oxygen tank and beg the judge not to throw her out onto the streets. Meanwhile, her grandmonsters were breeding pit bulls and charging an admittance fee for the dogfights they were having in the basement of our building. It didn't take us long to discover that we had made a huge mistake. Neither one of us had the skill set necessary to be slumlords. It simply wasn't our nature. We've gone on to successfully own other rental properties, but apartment buildings in a scary city didn't work out for us. The point is that following a road less traveled will open you up to potential failure, so be prepared to take a few hits along the way. Being the one brave enough to crawl out of the crab pot won't guarantee your success, but it will at least put you up at bat.

Remember, you have baskets that you need to work on filling, so if your current exchange rate isn't high enough to fund your baskets, explore ways to increase your rate of exchange. *The Millionaire Fastlane* by MJ DeMarco advocates and advises for a fast lane to success and describes entrepreneurship as the vehicle to get you to that success. The book is fabulous, and as an adviser to hundreds of self-employed people over many years, I couldn't agree more. Buyer beware though; self-employment is not an easy road that will guarantee your deliverance out of demanding work.

When teaching small business development classes for small business owners, we would always ask participants why they wanted to be business owners. The most often heard reasons were usually comments such as I only want to work when I feel like it, I don't want to have to listen to a boss, and I want to be able to buy a new car or other large purchase. Self-employment is one of the best ways to own your success, but plenty of the clients I've worked with don't have the aptitude for it. The ones that succeed work hard for it even when they don't feel like it and are committed to consistently delivering a quality product or service to the market. Being self-employed means you will have many bosses, and being successful at self-employment requires that you will listen to them all. You will still be working after your employees have left for the day, and the new car purchase will have to wait until after all your contractors, vendors, and employees have been paid. If you don't like dealing with paperwork or deadlines, think twice about starting your own business because hiring people to manage all those things will eat away at your bottom line.

On the other hand, if you are self-disciplined and willing to work hard, self-employment can give you a career with none of the traditional limits.

The good news is that you can have apples in more than one basket. For many people, a traditional job and a side hustle is the best way to fill their baskets. For others, it can be acquiring rental properties alongside their traditional job. A great diversified approach can be a combination of any of the following: a full-time job, side job, rental properties, or investment accounts. Some clients have become so successful at their side jobs they've been able to give up their full-time jobs. Others have made managing their real estate ventures a full-time gig. You will need to make sure you aren't spreading yourself too thin and neglecting to fulfill your obligations. It's entirely possible to plant so many trees that you don't have time to keep them fertilized and watered, only to watch them all dry up and wither away. Managed properly, however, spreading your time around might mean a faster exit plan to retirement as you are able to fund baskets you wouldn't be able to fill with just a regular job.

My own experiences and the work I've done with clients have given me some insight into the most successful methods of building wealth, and I'm going to share a few of them with you here.

Live below your means in the beginning. Buy the smaller house or the less expensive car. It's also okay to say no when your kids ask for the three-hundred-dollar sneakers. Most people live so far above their means that they subsidize their lifestyles with credit card debt and/or have no money left for savings. Practicing living below your means is a great lesson in learning to budget and save money. Saying no to those sneakers will teach your kids the value of money and the importance of not having to be just like everyone else. In the end, the *things* you acquire will be worth less than the vacations you saved for or the time you enjoy when you retire. Take a hard look at your income and develop a monthly budget so that you know what you have coming in and what needs to go out. These amounts need to balance, and when they don't, you will need to either increase money flowing in or decrease money flowing out. This part sucks, but the rewards will be worthwhile, so work through the process. Give yourself the opportunity to have some goals to work toward, and they can include things like the bigger house, the fast car, and the sneakers, but getting there is part of the journey. Work the process. Waiting to get these things when you can afford them allows you to really luxuriate in the satisfaction of having earned them. Don't deny yourself this pleasure!

Mind the small amounts. People have a tendency not to pay attention to small amounts, but a few dollars here and there add up over time. Businesses know that and prey on this weakness. That's why they pitch subscription plans or small ticket items that cost only a few dollars but slowly erode our ability to build wealth. Check your credit card statements for regularly occurring charges and analyze the cost-benefit analysis of these expenses. Stopping every morning for that indulgent coffee no longer feels special when you do it every day, but splurge once a week and it becomes a well-earned treat. One of the easiest ways to find money is to curb unnecessary spending.

The house—most of us have a goal of owning a home, and it's a worthwhile one. Unfortunately, though, too many people are in mortgages that are over their heads. Do not let the bank or the mortgage broker tell you how much of a mortgage you can afford. Read that last sentence again. You will need to do your own math to find a home with a price that is in a range you can be comfortable with. Finance your home for the shortest period you can afford and add to the payments whenever possible. I have too many clients in their seventies that still have large mortgages. It's a trend that's been developing over the last fifteen or so years, and it's sad to see people trapped in mortgages into their retirement years.

> Michelle called to discuss the potential purchase of a home she and her husband had seen. The price was steep, and I had big concerns about the mortgage, taxes, and insurance that would go along with the purchase. Michelle was in love with the house, though, so my concerns fell on deaf ears. Besides, she said, "The mortgage broker says we can afford the house." They purchased

the home in 2006. By 2008, the economy had collapsed, and her husband, a builder, was feeling the financial pinch in his business. The real estate bubble burst, and they couldn't even sell their house for what they had paid. Her husband was angry and blamed her for the home purchase. Eventually, the marriage crumbled around them, and the home was lost in foreclosure.

I've studied and read a lot written by financial experts, and there are different views on this topic. One well-known author advocates carrying enormous amounts of debt so that you are always using other people's money. This method does not work for me. My personal choice is to be debt-free or carry as little debt as possible. This is *my* choice and experience because having no debt makes *me* sleep better at night. Three years ago, my husband and I made the decision to withdraw money from one of our investment accounts to pay off our mortgage. It was a huge deal for us. We even drilled a hole in the top of our newel post (my husband's a handy guy), dropped our paid mortgage note in, and covered the hole with a carved petrified walrus mortgage plug. Like I said, it was a big deal! We then increased the amount of our monthly savings transfer to include the mortgage payment, with the goal of repaying the savings amount in three years. Pulling the money out of our savings was painful, but the satisfaction of having no mortgage was worth the temporary dip in our account. The good news is that we have replaced the original amount and continue to fund with the increased amount that included the mortgage payment. These additional funds are growing and bringing us closer to our retirement goals every day!

Retirement savings—save more than you think you can. This money needs to come directly out of your bank account through automatic monthly withdrawals. This is nonnegotiable. Most people have the general mindset that they will save whatever money they have left. Let me assure you that there will never be anything left. If you didn't get that sentence the first time, let me repeat it. There will never be anything left! That is one of the most basic laws of money. You will always spend whatever you have! Traditional retirement savings that promote saving less than ten percent of your earnings for retirement will not allow adequate retirement savings. At a minimum, you should try to double this amount and diversify it. Invest the maximum into an employer-funded retirement account, which uses pretax dollars, and invest the same amount into either a Roth or another posttax investment account. The Roth or posttax investment account will be available to you at retirement age with no tax consequences, so you can balance what you withdraw between pretax and posttax funds. Balancing how you withdraw these funds at retirement will allow you to keep your taxable income as low as possible, and this means you will pay less tax on your money in your retirement years. Fund retirement savings in a diversified method as quickly as you can with a goal of earlier retirement. Too many people work hard their entire lives for a retirement, and they die before they can enjoy it.

> My mother entered a postal career later in life. My father retired at fifty from the phone company, but my mother wanted to work long enough to have her own pension. She worked long hours and often seven days a week, but she was always watching the growth in her thrift saving plan. At sixty-three, she finally made the decision to retire. Six months later, she was diagnosed with ovarian cancer and died a month after her sixty-fifth birthday. She spent the last year and a half of her life struggling through surgery, chemotherapy, and doctor's appointments. Her retirement wasn't the future she had dreamed of.

Your potential to save will change as you move through different phases of your life. Many of the books I've read by experts are written by people without children. Most of us with children will find that our ability to work or save is significantly impacted during the years we are busy parenting and supporting children.

Even households with both parents working full-time will usually have high childcare expenses that impact their ability to save. It's not uncommon for me to do tax returns for clients that are paying fifteen thousand dollars or more per year in childcare expenses. Other situations, such as economic dips or a worldwide pandemic (still hard to believe I am writing this), will impact our ability to save as well. Some of my potentially highest earnings years were spent parenting. I don't regret that for a minute, but it's a factor worth considering. My best savings years were after my children were grown, and I had to ramp up my monthly savings amount to make up for some less productive years.

Give your money the gift of time. Tiny amounts of money invested periodically over the years will grow to become large amounts. Start by putting small amounts into the baskets you want to fund and then increase those amounts on a regular basis. You will be surprised to learn that you will not miss those monies, and watching those monies grow will give you the satisfaction you need to increase the amounts you are saving. It's so rewarding to watch your savings grow!

College savings and kids—if you have children, it's likely that one of your largest expenses will be paying for college. Fund a college savings plan such as a 529 plan through automatic monthly withdrawals starting when your children are young. Encourage other family members interested in giving Christmas or birthday gifts to your children to fund these plans as well. These plans can be rolled from one child to another child or family member in case one child doesn't use the funds. The initial investment and earnings are tax-free when used for education. Fund this account *after* you fund your own retirement account; starting off with smaller initial amounts is also fine. Do not sacrifice your own future for your kid's education. Counsel them regarding the costs of their education. Guidance counselors, though there to help, will not be the ones held liable for the tuition bills. College admission staff should be viewed as salespeople. Shop around for the best deal, and let your kids invest themselves in the cost of their education. I have far too many clients who have destroyed their financial future paying for their kid's college education.

> Mark and Sandy have three daughters. When it was time for their first daughter to attend college, they weren't prepared for the salesman-like hard sell and the pressure they felt. The college admissions people made them feel guilty when they asked questions about cost and made them feel like terrible parents who didn't want to pay for their daughter to get a good education. Once they were in debt for one daughter, they felt compelled to do the same for the second and third girls. In total, they amassed over three hundred thousand dollars in student loans. They are now retirement age but still struggling to manage their college debt.

I mentioned this earlier, but it bears repeating. Many financial experts do not have children, and having children is a game changer. Having children will require huge sacrifices, and one of the most challenging tasks you will have will be to teach them healthy money habits. Indulging them to the extent that you compromise your own future is not a lesson you want them to learn. Be realistic about your finances so that they learn the work required to get them the things they want. Too many people sacrifice their own future in the guise of fulfilling all their children's dreams, only to become dependent on their kids later in life. Give your children the gift of not having to worry about your financial future.

> David and Sally were blessed with only one child, and they showered this son with everything they had. They mortgaged their home and built an addition with a game and hangout room for him and all his friends. They had the most popular house in the neighborhood. When he started playing sports, they paid for coaching and equipment, racking up huge amounts of credit card debt. They took out a home-equity loan

and installed an in-ground pool for him to swim with his friends. When he developed an interest in sports memorabilia, they traveled all over the country, helping him build his collection, most of which they funded with even more debt. College came up so fast that they had no savings and financed his expensive education, and then there was the graduate program abroad at additional expense. They were too proud to tell him they were hurting financially. Their boy is married now and starting a family of his own, and he is pained to see that they are suffering financially. "Why didn't you ever say no?" he asked them.

Water your own garden first. Your kids will grow up and expect lives of their own. Do not burden them with the need to support you financially or emotionally. Eventually, your kids will move on and build their own lives, and you will be left with yours. Make sure that the life you are left with is the one you want to live.

- What baskets do you need to fund?

- Do you know what your exchange rate is?

- What are your dreams for retirement?

- Write a plan to fund your dreams.

Chapter 20
Two Heads Are Better than One

Between every two pines, there is a doorway to a new world.

—John Muir

In my twenty-ninth year, I found myself a single parent with two young girls. It was a surprisingly great year for me. My business was growing every day. I had started therapy and yoga, and I even bought my own house. It was a huge time of self-growth. I was enjoying the freedom of being on my own, and it was exciting to learn things about myself. Nine years in an abusive relationship had left little time for my own self-discovery.

There were guys interested in dating me, but I didn't trust myself to make a good decision, so a friend helped me develop an application to date Sherri Mahoney. I knew what things I was looking for in my next relationship, and having these things down on paper seemed like a map to finding the right guy. My list was clear, concise, and outlined exactly the type of tool-belt-wearing kind of guy I was looking for. I wasn't looking for someone to support me financially; heck, I was already doing that all on my own.

Bill entered the picture shortly thereafter. He met and excelled at all the fun-loving characteristics I had outlined on my application and had no trouble with my financial independence. In fact, he loved the fact that, as he said, I could bring home the bacon and fry it up in the pan. There was only one problem. Bill didn't have any bacon, and he wasn't making any. He was a single guy with no kids, making just enough money to pay for his skiing and sailing adventures. I was the only one making the bacon. It didn't take me long to realize I was going to have to do a quick rewrite on my application because the person I needed in my life at least needed to be able to support himself. Bill wasn't pleased with me changing the terms of our arrangement. He had never had to worry about supporting himself before, and it seemed a little bit of a bait and switch to him. I wasn't willing to compromise on this issue, though, and he had to make some difficult changes. Luckily, he had started his own therapy and was able to see the holes in his "fun all the time theory" that left his world in financial chaos. The journey of him owning his own financial success had begun.

We've been fortunate to have a therapist with us along for the ride who is a partner in our success. He helps us manage our emotional baggage so that we can focus on building a relationship that supports each of us in healthy ways. Therapy has allowed us to take our broken bits and build a healthy relationship, something of which we were initially weary. Many years of therapy have gifted us with the ability to fine-tune our goals and learn how to work together effectively as a team. We aren't always successful at working together effectively, but therapy has helped us identify the talents and skill sets that we each bring to the table. Mechanically, Bill is the builder of my dreams, and I'm the wealth builder. We've learned how to maximize the skills we each bring to the table. In equal turns, we are dreaming and building, supporting each other's dreams in the ways we each know how.

We've discovered that two people working effectively toward common goals can provide amazing results. Trust me, it hasn't been an easy journey. There have been plenty of bitter arguments and periods of time in our relationship where we simply couldn't get past ourselves enough to get on the same page or in agreement about difficult issues. Two different people will always have alternate ideas and views on any situation. Sometimes, we left therapy sessions so angry we would spend the whole ride home too frustrated to even look at each other. The difficulties in our relationship, though, have all been part of the journey that has made us stronger as a team. In retrospect, we couldn't always see that, and that has been part of our journey as well.

Two years into our relationship, I ended it. I simply wasn't willing to support Bill financially, and he was still struggling in a family business that was making no money. The struggle to break out of the crab pot was difficult, and his family saw no reason for him to make any changes in his life. They preferred to see him alone versus challenging the broken family dynamics. Since his family was angry at him and I was resolute that making a living be a condition of our relationship, Bill had no place to go. He set up a tent in my backyard while he figured things out. My youngest daughter, Casey, was unhappy with the breakup and would often visit and hang with him in the tent. The breakup, though, was exactly the wake-up call he needed to make changes, and within a month, he left the failing family business and had an excellent job. His family was not happy with him, but it was an amazing turnaround that opened an entirely new world for him. Casey was so excited to have him back in the picture that she performed a mock wedding ceremony in our kitchen, dressing him in his golf shoes with a sock tie and serving us apple juice in paper cups. It wasn't until she said, "Okay, you can kiss her now," that we finally realized she was marrying us. One of the requirements on my application was that the man I chose be good for my children, and Bill was amazing with both girls. He was the dream maker. Shortly thereafter, we had a real wedding, giving Casey the security and sense of permanence she so obviously wanted in her life.

You see, left to my own devices, I would just work and save all my money. Bill, left on his own, would have no retirement. Somewhere along the way, we've found a way to temper his "play all the time" attitude with my "let's get some work done" attitude. I'm not sure that we could have gotten here without therapy. We didn't have the best examples, and the maps we'd been given were paths made up of bitter relationships written by unhappy people. We wanted to follow a different road.

We've planted a lot of seeds. Some have flourished, and some have withered and died. From time to time, we still turn to each other and ask, "Are we being an effective team?"

In 2008, Bill and I found ourselves in an economic recession, stuck with two apartment buildings that we couldn't sell in a dismal real estate market. The tenants were out of work and not paying rent. Most of them did so much damage that it was easier to just pay the mortgages and keep the few decent tenants we had. It was one disaster after another, and I couldn't sleep at night for stressing over the problems we were having with these apartment buildings. Finally, amid a busy tax season, I said to Bill, "Please don't tell me one more horrible thing about them." True to my request, I heard little from him about the buildings over the next few months. I spoke with a client, a therapist, who gave me a piece of sage advice. She said, "You know, anything will sell if the price is low enough, and sometimes, peace of mind is worth more than financial gain." After accepting the fact that we would have to take a large hit on the sale, we relisted the properties at rock-bottom prices and finally were able to get rid of them. After tax season, Bill said, "Remember how you said not to tell you anything else bad about those buildings." He pulled out his iPhone and googled one of the addresses. Apparently, following a party in one of the apartments, someone had been shot and killed outside our building. There were dozens of news articles and clips of reporters showing footage outside our building. Bill had gone there to do plumbing work the day after the shooting, and reporters had been there reporting on the story. He told them he was just the plumber there to repair a leak. He waited months until after tax season had ended to share the story. He knew I couldn't bear to hear any more bad news about those buildings. We were an effective team! Just last year, my oldest daughter gave me a book about the city where we owned the properties titled *Murder and Mayhem*, and the book included the story about the murder at our building. Years later, we were finally able to laugh about what a disaster the apartments had been. Owning them taught us a lot. We learned what our tolerances were and highlighted some of our deficiencies. It required some major teamwork as we rehabbed buildings and dealt with difficult tenants. It also showed us another way of life and made us grateful that we were on a different path than our tenants.

Last year, the most amazing pumpkins seeded themselves and grew out of a pile of manure behind our barn. It was a great reminder that sometimes, being in a shitty place will force you to grow something beautiful. One of our deciding factors in moving and starting our farm in Westport was its proximity to our apartment buildings. Living in Westport has brought us a life of horses, sheep, donkeys, chickens, lavender, and peacocks. My husband and I have both built successful businesses in this town. Our daughters found spouses and are raising their children here on farms of their own. Owning those buildings may have been difficult, but it was part of the journey that got us to where we are now. Sometimes, when we are struggling, it helps to remind ourselves that this too shall pass. Tomorrow will be a different day, and what pains us today will be the stories of our lives that we laugh at down the road.

Traveling through life with a partner is not a necessity because we are all enough on our own. Personally, though, I have found that two heads working toward common goals can make the journey more interesting and your load a bit lighter. Find a partner that you can build a life with, but don't stay with a partner that holds you down. Life is too short for that, and most of us don't have closets large enough to hold a life's worth of emotional pain.

- Are you and your partner an effective team?

Part 3

Reaping What You Sow

Chapter 21

Have Faith, but Do Not Let Go of the Wheel

> Hope is like a bird that senses the dawn and carefully starts to sing while it is still dark.
>
> —Unknown

Whenever I read a book, I know that the book I am currently reading is the book I am meant to be reading at that particular time in my life. It's a little thing, I know, but important at the same time. Books have directed and guided me through certain chapters and times in my life and have given me many of the answers I was seeking at precisely the time I needed the answer. I've learned to have faith that when I open a book and begin to read, it will bring exactly what I need into my world that day. At times, it can take one or even two people to suggest a book before I purchase it. Other times, a friend will gift me a book. Either way, the book is now in my hands, but it means absolutely nothing until I make the decision to open the cover. Faith may have planted that book in the right place, but unless I read it, the book is nothing more than a pile of paper.

There is a great story that goes like this: a person is ranting at God and says that they have put all their prayers and faith in God for him to provide but that God has let them down. God responds that he heard the prayers and that he provided exactly the things they needed. He provided them with fertile soil, seeds, sun, and rain. All the person had to do was grow the things they wanted with the tools God had provided.

The fact is that we've all been given the tools we need to succeed. Whether we decide to pick them up and work with them will be our decision to own. Faith alone will not get you to success; picking up the gifts you've been given and using them will point you toward the success you desire. So have faith in the fact that what you've been given is enough to get you the life of your dreams and have the everlasting drive to pick up what you have and get to work. You are the one that will need to drive yourself to success.

A fast track to disappointment is giving away the keys to your success. I cannot begin to tell you how many clients I have worked with that have stories about how they trusted their spouse or partner to manage their finances. They often go something like this: "It was my responsibility to manage the household and raise the kids. My partner was supposed to oversee our finances." Someone in business will say, "I hired someone to manage my front end, and I can't believe they've been stealing money from me all these years." A business partner will come in and lament that his role was to manage marketing and development, and his partner was in charge of managing the money. The common denominator among them all is that they gave away control of their future.

> Lisa called me to discuss issues she was having with her husband. He was a stockbroker, and many of their friends, as well as her parents and brother, had invested money with him. There was some sort of investigation going on, but he kept telling her not to worry. It was about some other people at work. Nothing to do with him. She knew something wasn't right though. Eventually, he was brought up on criminal charges, and things really started unraveling. She found out that most of what he'd been telling her was a bunch of lies and that he had forged her signature and pulled all the equity out of their home

in an attempt to keep things afloat. She began divorce proceedings, but there wasn't much left of their financial life by the time he was found guilty. His retirement account was liquidated to make restitution to the people he had embezzled money from, and he had invested all their own money in his get rich scheme. He went off to spend a few years in jail, and she was left with two kids, a mortgage she couldn't afford, and a pile of bills. "I trusted him to take care of us," she kept saying over and over again.

Not every story ends as badly as this one, but it's important to participate in the decisions that impact you and be in the driver's seat of your own life. Letting go of the wheel can make you a casualty in someone else's wreckage.

Sometimes, it isn't even intentional. I've had many clients who have lost spouses to death or divorce only to discover that their spouses weren't so great at managing their finances. Often, we make the mistake of assuming that our partner or spouse has everything under control when, in fact, they might not have all the skills necessary to manage your joint finances. Your faith in that person alone won't make them great at managing your future. You will need to spend some time behind the wheel yourself to make sure that things are on track.

Have faith that the opportunities you need will present themselves, and know that without you taking the necessary steps to make things happen, you will not get the results you are looking for.

In February 2016, my youngest daughter called and asked what I thought about her and her boyfriend buying a house. She was twenty-four. I told her I thought it was a great idea. A week or two later, I sent her a listing for a house. "No," she said, "we want a house with more land." Her future father-in-law researched the house I had sent her the listing on and discovered that it actually had twelve acres, and the listing was incorrect. It was listed far under value based on the amount of land. There were few properties for sale in our town, and I was afraid it would be a competitive sale. Her boyfriend looked at the house with my husband and me, and there were cars lined up with potential buyers. The very next day, my daughter and her boyfriend wrote a letter saying why they believed they should own the home and made an offer over the asking price. There were ten other offers. They moved into their new home in April. She had faith that they would find a home, but without their efforts, they would have lost the home to another buyer.

Our oldest daughter used a similar tactic when she and her spouse bought their home. Due to the scarcity of houses in our town, she wrote letters to owners whenever she saw dumpsters or other indications that someone was renovating or moving out of a home. As full-time farmers, it was important that the house be near the farm they already owned, and sure enough, eventually, her letter found them a home just a few miles down the road from their farm. She had noticed a dumpster in front of the house, and the owner, recently deceased, had been an older farmer that had sold produce to them at their farm. Due to her efforts, the house never even hit the real estate market, and her family found a new home.

Faith will put opportunities in your path, and only you can decide whether to take that seed and plant it into the soil.

- Do you have faith that you will be given opportunities?

- Are you willing to do the work to make those opportunities happen in your life?

- When have you taken control of a situation and gotten a positive result that you were looking for?

Chapter 22
Pushing through the Fear

*Remember that the minute you take your first
step into the life of your dreams, the first to greet
you, there will be fear. Nod. Keep walking.*

—Brianna Wiest

Fear has always had a way of finding its way into my bed on the eve of my life's greatest successes. Sometimes, he will even move in weeks before the event. He stinks up my bedroom while I am trying to sleep, planting in my head reasons why my beautiful plans are doomed for failure. Sometimes, I can't evict him no matter how much I try.

In 2000, Bill and I were newly married, and my oldest daughter, Meg, who was twelve years old at the time, was dreaming of owning a horse. We lived in a small house on one-half acre of land. There was no room for a horse which meant that if she got a horse, we would need to pay board. She found a horse locally. "Let's just go see him," she said. The arena where she rode him for the first time was so filled with dust that I could barely see my hand in front of my face, but do you know what I could see from the other side of the indoor arena? Meg's white teeth that shone in the biggest smile I had ever seen. I knew we were in trouble. I had lunch with a friend, also my business coach, and lamented my tale of indecision. Meg had dreamed of horses her entire young life, but boarding a horse was ridiculously expensive. More than a car payment, I whined. My friend reminded me that there were other things in life of value besides money and to have faith that we would make things work out. Bill, of course, had long since been won over to the side of acquiring the horse. Remember, he was the dream maker. I was the scrooge. Owning a horse scared the crap out of me. There was the expense, yes, but there was another entirely different fear. Meg had been severely injured at five years old when a pony we owned stepped on her head, leaving her with five skull fractures. I agonized over the decision. Finally, I agreed, and Meg got the horse of her dreams.

Our adventures with Brownie had begun. Meg and I would go to the barn every afternoon so she could groom and attempt to ride him. At only six years old and a rescue from the racetrack, he had just about every bad trait you could imagine. Not a great racehorse, he had been starved at the track and suffered from neglect, so at feeding time would back himself into the corner of the stall baring his teeth at us. He would often rear up, smashing his head into the rafters of the stall. Before she could even attempt to ride him, she would lunge him on a line in a ring where he would run in a circle, leaning so far sideways, and at such a speed, I feared for her life. Only after being fully exhausted was he able to be ridden. A few weeks after we purchased him, we went to the barn Christmas night to introduce him to some family members. We found him lying on his side, foaming at the mouth and writhing in pain. He was extremely sick. It required a trailer ride to Tufts Veterinary Hospital, and we discussed having to take out a home-equity loan just to pay the veterinary bills. Time passed, and both Meg and I learned how to manage Brownie's demanding health needs. Meg and Brownie forged a bond stronger than any I had ever witnessed, and Meg blossomed as both a young woman and a rider. She loved her time at the barn, and Brownie was the light of her life. Brownie grew older, became calmer and more playful, and was by Meg's side until he died of old age just a few years ago. We were all heartbroken to see him go. The role he played in developing Meg's character was one I could never put a price on, and I was glad that I had pushed through my fears to give her the experience of owning him. He also played a big part in getting us to an even bigger and more fearful chapter in our lives.

In 2004, Casey, our younger daughter, asked if she could also get a horse. Boarding one horse was expensive, but boarding two would be the cost of a mortgage. Bill, ever the dream maker, asked, "But how do you get one a horse and tell the other no?" He came home from work one day and said that we should take a road trip to Westport, a small farming town not too far from Cape Cod, where we lived. We headed off to Newport for the weekend with Meg in the back seat, passing through Westport on our way. Our plan was always to find a place with a little more land when the girls were grown. Moving them while they were in school didn't seem like an option. From the back seat, looking at the beautiful farmland, Meg rallied, "What do you mean, you're finally going to get a house with some land after we're grown? I want to move now." On our way back from Newport, a realtor suggested we look at a piece of land that was for sale.

"You will need to have some imagination," she said. "It needs a lot of work." The land was located down a long private driveway. It had been a gravel pit, so it was barren and ugly. Not a blade of grass, piles of old stumps, debris, and old tires had been dumped everywhere, and when the wind blew, the air was filled with enough blowing dirt that you could feel it coat your teeth. Meg and Bill instantly had visions of a house on a hill with a view of the river and a barn for the horses. We made a lowball offer I was sure would get rejected (fingers crossed), and when the offer was surprisingly accepted (punch to the gut), my old friend, fear, set up permanent residence in my bed.

"I have a successful accounting practice, and Bill has an excellent job," I argued. Despite my objections, the sale of our current home and purchase of the twenty-five acres of barren, not-so-farmable land began to slide forward at an easy pace. I expressed my fears to Meg about our house selling.

"Don't worry," she said, "the house will sell." It sold for a ridiculously high amount of money, just a week after being on the market, and the house where we had been boarding our two horses became vacant and in need of a tenant. We moved in during the building process, and the girls had the time of their lives bonding with their horses. They spent more time in the barn than they did in the house.

Bill and I were ridiculously busy building the house. Bill was doing all the plumbing, and even though we were building a modular home, we were finishing the inside ourselves and using local subcontractors that were clients of mine. At night, I was sewing curtains in the rental house and picking out wallpaper I would hang before our move-in date. There was a moving truck scheduled for June 13, so it was a firm deadline. The pony we had purchased for Casey had traveled up from an Amish farm in Virginia, and she was a sweet little round thing named Ginger. One week we had checkup visits from both the vet and the farrier to have her feet trimmed. They both commented on her weight gain and suggested we cut back on her hay. That Friday, April 24, Earth Day, the girls were in the house, putting pictures in their horse photo albums and noticed something in the paddock with the horses that looked like a pile of hay. There were two other horses boarding at the barn, and surprisingly, all four horses were lying down on the ground. The girls ran down to the barn and found that Ginger had given birth to a beautiful little filly. She had come to us pregnant, and her roundness had concealed the tiny seed she was growing inside. Dakota's birth was the talk of the town, and before long, there was an ambulance and lines of cars down the road. Word spread quickly about her miraculous birth, and everyone wanted to come meet her. Dakota was spoiled from the minute she was born. Every night, we would all sit in her stall and take turns pulling her onto our laps, where we would massage her little body from her nose to her tail. We laughed at her antics in the paddock as she would try to run and often crash into water buckets or trip over her own feet. Having a third horse meant our move to Westport, where we would have our own barn, made perfect sense. We moved up the deadline to build the barn since Dakota was too young to be out in the elements without shelter and would be an easy mark for coyotes. On June 13, a large trailer backed up to the rental house, and the two horses walked on. Little Dakota easily jumped up, following her mother. Our journey to Westport and our adventures in building a farm were about to begin.

Time and experience have taught me that when fear crawls into my bed at night, I push back hard because I have found that the things in life I have feared the most have often brought the most joy. Are you afraid, dear reader? Push back hard at your fears with all your might! You are stronger than you know.

- What fears keep you up at night?

- How can you push through your fears?

Chapter 23
Manifesting Your Dreams

To plant a garden is to believe in tomorrow.

—Audrey Hepburn

Create the highest, grandest vision possible for your life because you become what you believe.

—Oprah Winfrey

A key secret to manifesting your dreams is to design and develop a clear vision of them. In my home, I've discovered that pictures held to my refrigerator by magnets usually have a way of manifesting themselves in reality. One year, I admired a picture of a pair of boots in a magazine and stuck the picture on our fridge. That Christmas, they were under the tree. There was an image of a pool in a garden setting with chickens strutting nearby that struck me as beautiful, and I stuck that image to the refrigerator. I had a vision of my husband and me swimming in the summers with our grandchildren in that pool. Years later, we installed a pool surrounded by gardens in our backyard, and last year two chickens, Pearl and Henrietta, rescued from the advances of the barnyard roosters, found their way into our pool area, where they entertained us all and ate table scraps. It was funny to realize how close the picture in our yard resembled the one that had hung on our refrigerator for so many years. Another picture of a meditation garden hung there for a couple of years before becoming a reality two years ago.

One year, shortly after my mother's death, my husband and I drove to Florida with my father. I spent the long ride studying lavender fields and growing techniques. Our barren land was now fields of green but lacked the dense nutrients to grow most crops. A picture in a magazine of land alongside salt marshes resembled ours, and the article that accompanied it said that the soil presented perfect growing conditions for lavender. The seed was planted in my mind, and that spring, we planted two fields of lavender. The lavender was too much to cut and consume, and summers found me driving between farm stands with my jeep full of buzzing bees and baskets of lavender. I had a vision of people coming to our farm to see the fields and cut their own lavender bunches. That summer, over two hundred people visited our small farm to cut lavender and see the gardens, and the following summer, we hosted over six hundred guests. The funny thing was, I had seen all this in my head long before it happened.

I dreamed and had visions of sheep, peacocks, and donkeys, and where faith grew, ideas germinated, and plans were made. Hard work made these dreams become a reality, and the people that visit our farm each year bring their children to see the animals that now make our farm their home.

My daughter once told me that when you ride a horse, you are always looking ahead at the next turn or the next jump. By the time the horse and rider get there, the action has already been performed in your mind's eye. Your eyes are seeing the smooth execution of the maneuver before you ask the horse to perform it. The horse senses your confidence in the completion of the action and smoothly performs each time. The vision of the rider has driven the horse to success, and the horse and rider are perfectly aligned. Our dreams and our visions are like that.

Writing this book has been my dream for many years, and in my vision, I was sitting in a cabin in the mountains of New Hampshire with snow gently falling outside the windows writing this book. We owned a small house in Florida that we loved, but the energy there was not the energy I needed to author this book. We sold the home, and in a huge leap of faith, we rolled the proceeds into an account earmarked for a like-kind exchange to potentially defer taxes on the gain from the sale. We had been looking for a cabin in the mountains for months, and there was nothing on the market. People had been leaving the cities in record numbers and purchasing homes in remote areas due to COVID. Prices were high, and availability was exceedingly low. We had only forty-five days to find a property. I met with a client in my Cape Cod office who had also been looking for a property. I was surprised to find that he knew the remote area where we were looking. He had finally given up his search and settled on a piece of land since he hadn't been able to find a cabin. He told me that he was still getting emails for new listings and would pass along anything he found. A couple of weeks later, on a Friday, I received an email from him about a house that had just been listed. The asking price plus necessary furnishings was precisely the amount of the proceeds from the sale of our Florida home. It was a chalet-style mountain home in exactly the town we had been looking. I forwarded the email to my husband, who suggested we drive up the next day. There were a lot of interested buyers, and realtors were there doing virtual showings to clients in other parts of the country. We stayed so long looking at the house that the owners eventually came back, and the listing agent introduced us. The owner was a builder and happy to talk to another contractor. He was also happy to know that we knew the area well and had previously lived close by. We made our offer that afternoon, and today, just a few months later, I write to you from the cabin in the woods that filled my vision. There is a fire glowing softly in the woodstove beside me, and outside, the woods are full of dusk and snow. My next vision is starting to percolate.

I am here to tell you that you can build the life you dream of. Paint a picture so rich that you can see, feel, and taste every element of it. Build the vision. See it. Feel it. Taste it. Experience it—while you are folding laundry, before you go to bed, when you brush your teeth, in the morning when you do your affirmations. Manifest that incredible dream every single frigging day until you make that dream happen.

- What dreams would you like to manifest in your life?

- What does the vision of your dream life look like?

Chapter 24
Growing Your Financial Success

It always seems impossible until it's done.

—Nelson Mandela

How do we define financial success? We are flooded with information daily. Television ads, social media, and magazine pictures with photos of beautiful people in amazing places are all developed in a thinly disguised attempt to illustrate what success is. Do you think a woman wearing a size zero, bright red evening gown in stiletto heels, lounging on a multimillion-dollar yacht, holding a glass of champagne, is a vision of success? I don't think so. She's a manipulative tool, put there to sell you jewelry, perfume, or some other piece of bling with no guarantee of happiness included in the sale. The model in that lovely dress kicks off those toe-gnawing heels the minute she walks away from the camera and rushes home so she can throw on a comfortable pair of sweatpants and take off her bra.

My husband and I often go to Newport, Rhode Island, and watch the parade of people that flood the area at night. Early in the evening, the young women in their short dresses and high heels are all laughing and strutting as they parade their way up and down the street. Just a few short hours later, the street tells a different story. We see the same groups of women dragging themselves along. The strut has turned into a crawl, and many of them are limping and feeling a burning in their toes I know oh so well. The glamour of their outfits has faded, the alcohol is running the show, and the bed is starting to look better than even Tom Cruise right now. It's the best show in town!

Only we can decide what financial success means to us. Don't rely on social media and advertisements, designed with the sole intent of milking you of your hard-earned dollars, to be the catalyst that drives your definition of success. Spend time getting to understand yourself and develop a feeling deep in your soul for the things that bring you joy. Financial success starts with a dream. Develop the vision of your dreams and paint that vision in your head a hundred times a day. As for the fears and toxic people that rush in with the intent of raining on your parade, push those festering, undermining turds out the door.

> Dennis came to me with plans to open a dry-cleaning business. The fact that he claimed to never have washed even a pair of socks made me wonder about his path, but he pursued it. The franchise he purchased was turnkey, and soon he was open for business. He set up shop in a brand-new plaza next to a grocery store and was soon remarkably busy. His current wife decided she wasn't in love with him or the business, and they divorced shortly after he opened shop. He married a woman a few years later that loved him and loved to do laundry. When the town passed zoning bylaws and restrictions that started to affect his ability to use the necessary dry-cleaning chemicals, he set up commercial washers and dryers in the basement of his home and started sending his shirts out to other dry-cleaning vendors. Besides, he told me, most people don't read the labels on their clothes. The labels usually specify no dry-cleaning, and the dry-cleaning solvents are bad for your skin. Every day, Dennis and his wife would open the store, collect the clothes, and bring them home to wash and press in the base-

ment of their home. His customers raved about his dry-cleaning service. I worked with Dennis and his wife for over twenty years until they sold their business and retired to their condominium on the beach in South Carolina. They had made a plan for their financial success, rewritten it as needed, and were living their dream!

Have faith that your dreams for financial success are possible, and know that you will do the work to make them happen. Develop a mantra that you repeat before bed, first thing in the morning, and during the day that supports your dreams. Financial success is there for you to own, and the right mindset is the tool that will get you there.

My husband and I own two homes of significant value with no mortgages, our debt load is light, and we have filled our home with beautiful things. Not everything we own is of huge financial value, but they are things that have meaning to us. Someday, when the work of maintaining or dusting these things distracts us from the joy in our days, we will shed many of those things and lighten our load. We have retirement accounts and savings accounts, and someday soon, we will have enough in these accounts to retire. We struggle with wondering how much we need to retire and how much longer we need to work. My mother's early death reminds me that a long life is not a guarantee, but I counter that with the fear of not having enough to sustain a retirement. By many examples, we are successful, and yet I know many people with far more in the bank than us. Those people, though, aren't even in our race. Time and health are the colors of the horses in our race, and eventually, they will outrun us. We have built and followed a map that is bringing us to our own definition of success. Money is not the goal. Options are the goal, and the goal is to have options that allow us to enjoy the things we love. The options to go to the places in our dreams, the luxury of time spent with our grandkids, and the resources to take them places are the options we dream of, and the money we accumulate is the means to realize those options. Our dreams have been rewritten, and our paths modified when life has thrown surprises at us. We purchased and enjoyed a home in Florida where we planned to spend time in the winters after our retirement, but then we rewrote that plan. The mountains in New Hampshire, where I had grown up and where we spent the early years of our relationship, called us home, and a vision of a home nestled among pines began to take seed. Our time living with COVID has reminded us that we have more simplistic roots. Our journey goes on, but our path has changed direction in order to meet our current needs.

The financial success of our dreams is there for each of us, and the only limitations placed on obtaining it are those we place on ourselves. The walls that keep our success away are built with our own hands; burn them down! Define your success, get your mind in the right place, develop habits that support your success, push away your doubts and fears, and reach for your success. Reach and stretch for it with every ounce of will and faith that you have inside yourself, and then do the work, the hard work, to make it happen. The seeds to grow your financial success rest in the palm of your hand, and the soil is waiting. Plant them.

- What is your definition of financial success?

- What does your dream of financial success look like?

- Write a map to reach your goals of financial success.

Chapter 25
The Right Balance

> For everything, there is a season, a time for every activity under heaven. A time to be born and a time to die. A time to plant and a time to harvest.
>
> —Ecclesiastes 3:1–8 (NLT)

In 2009, we had been living in Westport for a few years and were working on the seemingly never-ending process of building our farm. I was working my accounting practice from my original office on Cape Cod and from a small office building we had built across the driveway from our home in Westport. I joined a group of business owners, many of whom were struggling to start or grow their businesses. At one of our meetings, we spent two emotional hours where everyone vented about their difficulties trying to balance building their businesses along with their personal lives. Many of the people in the group had young children and were having difficulties finding childcare that would allow them to work. One woman had two aging parents and was trying to care for them while building her business.

My life was different from the women with young children, but I clearly remember the days of trying to juggle client meetings in between caring for my daughters. The day my youngest daughter started full-day kindergarten was bittersweet but also a blessing in the relief it provided me regarding my ability to work without worrying about childcare. One day, in particular, my assistant had called out sick, and the school called to tell me that my daughter was sick and needed to be picked up from school. I had an appointment with a client scheduled that day but was unable to reach the client by phone prior to running out the door. I left a note on the door stating that there had been an emergency, but the client was not understanding and berated me for being unprofessional. It was a stinging blow that I still carry with me. In the early days of my career, balancing my work with caring for two daughters was always a challenge.

One day, I visited a friend in her early sixties. I was thirty at the time. We chatted and walked while admiring her beautiful gardens. I bemoaned my lack of time to garden and wondered about her ability to find the time to create such wondrous gardens. She gave me some incredibly sage advice. "You see," she explained, "this is my season to garden." Her children were grown, and she finally had the time to create the gardens of which she had always dreamed. She told me that in a few short years, my own children would be grown and that I, too, would have beautiful gardens. I reflect back on those wise words often. The days of my daughters playing at my feet are gone, and my daughters have children of their own. My gardens are lovely; it is my season to garden.

Our lives are made up of seasons—a time to play, a time to grow, a time to work, a time to garden. Find the balance in whatever season you are currently in. They will all pass much too fast.

My mother died before living her last season. She worked a crazy schedule spending her life too exhausted to enjoy her days and was dedicated to saving enjoyment for her retirement years. Her death had a significant impact on the way I started to look at my days. I wasn't willing to trade a life of nothing but work for the glimmer of a retirement dream. I still struggle to find the balance and push myself to say yes to things that bring enjoyment to every day. I know that retirement is not a guarantee.

Ovarian cancer is hereditary, so when my mother was diagnosed, my own doctor asked to have my mother tested for the BRCA1 and BRCA2 genes. Her reasoning was that if my mother was a carrier of those variants, it would be better to have her tested for my own health insurance reasons. It would give me the opportunity to pursue genetic counseling. Interestingly, my mother tested negative for those variants, and a few years ago, I did my own test to see if I had the variants. I also tested negative, and while that does give me some hope of a fate different than my mother's early death, I still worry. Just a few days ago, my best friend from childhood messaged me to say that she had recently been diagnosed with advanced colon cancer, and my heart was aching. Life always finds a way to remind me to treasure my days.

Find your balance in work and in life. Live in your season, whatever season that might be. Stop wishing and waiting for your babies to grow up. They will soon enough, and you will miss your days with them. Enjoy your parents while they're alive. Their seasons will probably end before yours. Plan for your future, but remember to live, love, laugh and enjoy each day. There are pleasures to be discovered in every season.

- Do you struggle to find balance in your life?

- Are you enjoying the season your life is in right now?

- Can you see how your life evolves through different seasons?

Chapter 26
Less Really Is More!

Simplicity is the ultimate sophistication.

—Leonardo da Vinci

Five years ago, at a therapy session, we discussed with our therapist the philosophy that less is more. I knew there was something important in this message for me, so I wrote that mantra on a sticky note and attached it to my desk. I looked at that sticky note regularly and moved it around when I cleaned my desk, smoothing down its frayed edges. When the note faded, I rewrote it on a bigger sticky note, moving it to the center of my desk. I knew the message was important. I read that note daily. I struggled to find reasons for wanting less. I told my husband that I was having trouble with the concept. "I don't know," I told him. "I think more is more, and I like more better." My business was continuing to grow, we had a rental house in Florida to manage, and life was so busy. We had farm animals to care for, dozens of beautiful gardens, lavender fields, and life seemed to be about doing more and more. My type-A personality meant I was having a tough time slowing down. The girls were in houses of their own, and I was enjoying some renovation projects in our own home. Our home was becoming more beautiful every day. People exposed to trauma in their childhoods often feel a need to prove themselves and have trouble slowing down. Intellectually, I knew this about myself, but wasn't more just better and better? It's an argument I still have with myself almost every day.

When the world shut down in the spring of 2020, it brought things into focus. Suddenly, all the errands and shopping I thought I had to do wasn't even an option. Eating out also wasn't an option. We, along with everyone else, discovered that we could get by with less, and I found myself glimpsing the reality that less can actually be more. More time for other kinds of pleasures. Long, lazy afternoons and nights when we weren't rushing around. A natural homebody, I'm sad to say that part of me enjoyed this slower pace. I drove my vehicle less than five thousand miles that year. I started making relishes and jellies again that summer and had a sourdough starter burping on my counter. Our gardens were beautiful that year.

The farms in our town were busier than ever. People wanted local produce grown by the farmers that they trusted in our community. When we had our lavender event that year, over six hundred people came for the simple pleasure of cutting bunches of lavender and taking pictures in the fields. We were all suddenly discovering the small wonders that exist all around us. The funny thing is that most of us weren't suffering. In fact, our days seemed richer and more filled with beauty than they had before. The flowers that year seemed more brilliant than ever to behold. While the people in the cities might not have had the space and the same opportunities that existed in our little farm community, life in our town was rich. Ironically, it seemed like the places with less were really, after all, the places with more.

COVID separated us from our daughters and grandchildren, and that was painful. We missed months of our granddaughter's life when she was a baby, a time we will never get back. But it brought us closer too. After the quarantine period, we implemented weekly family dinners, and where our time together might have once been taken for granted, we now treasure the value of those dinners. Our daughters reminisced about their time spent growing up in the mountains of New Hampshire and asked us to look for a cabin in the woods so that their children could have the same experiences they had enjoyed with us at my father's cabin in the mountains. We were all craving simpler times.

These days, I'm pushing toward some different goals. In my morning meditation, I'm holding onto the vision of a life where less really is more. The trees outside our mountain cabin are covered with snow, and there is a voice in my head that whispers in my ear. "Slow down," the voice says. "Less is more," it whispers. I take a deep, slow breath, look at the snow outside the window, and remind myself that less really is more.

- Do you believe that less is more?

- Can you do things to slow down your days?

- What experiences have taught you to enjoy less being more?

Chapter 27

Love Will Always Defeat Common Sense and Sound Financial Advice

Money is numbers, and numbers never end. If it takes money to be happy, your search for happiness will never end.

—Robert Nesta Marley

Don't judge each day by the harvest you reap but by the seeds that you plant.

—Robert Louis Stevenson

I've noticed an interesting trajectory while working with clients. A client will call to set up a meeting to discuss a critical issue. They claim to want to know the right financial answer to the question being posed. Should we sell the house? Buy the house? Take the money out of retirement for the vacation? Move closer to the kids? The questions are varied, but consistently one truth prevails. We can debate the facts and the tax consequences, but emotions and love are what will really drive their decision. Sometimes, a tax or financial consequence might delay or modify the event, but we always develop a plan that will minimize the impact and find a way for them to follow their hearts.

Many years spent collaborating with clients have taught me that to be effective, I must listen with my ears and respond with my heart.

This practice has served me well because pushing an agenda with only a monetary consequence would leave me frustrated with clients who know in their hearts what they really want. My role becomes more aligned with a client's needs when I give them permission to follow their hearts and find a way to minimize the impact their choices will have on their future financial situation.

> Judy called me to review her plan to pull money from her retirement account to fund a massive remodel of her home. She needed a significant amount of money, and pulling out that large of an amount in one year would mean that much of the amount would be taxed in higher tax brackets. She told me that she knew it seemed foolish. She had lived in her house for many years and gotten by just fine. She was in her mid-sixties, though, and tired of living in a house she didn't love. She wanted to gut the home and turn it into the house of her dreams. Her kids were not happy with her plans. "The house is fine the way it is," they told her. "You're going to run out of money to live on," they said. Judy knew how much money she had, and she knew that she would still have a significant amount of money even after paying for the remodel. She wanted to stay in the house but didn't want to stay in the house the way it was. The tax implications of drawing such a large amount out of retirement all at once were daunting, but I knew that Judy knew what she wanted. We worked together and devised a plan so that she could spread the distributions out over three years by pulling funds from an existing home-equity line with very low interest. By spreading the distribution out over three years, we were able to significantly reduce the tax implications. Judy completed her remodel and loved every minute

of living in her beautifully remade home. As a tax accountant, I could have crushed her dreams by highlighting the tax mistakes of the retirement distribution, but listening to her dreams and helping her achieve them served her much better.

Sometimes, a client will be holding back on deciding because their head is telling them one thing, but in their heart, they know it's not a good fit. The challenge we face often involves understanding ourselves enough to know what we want, and it's not always easy to identify that. We have so many outside influences pushing and pulling us in different directions that it can be hard to hear our own internal voices. And even when we identify what we want, there is the internal friction of the voice in our head telling us why our plan is not financially sound or doomed for failure. Sometimes, the struggle we experience lies within ourselves.

A few years ago, one of our young lambs got her head stuck in one of the square holes that make up our sheep fence. She had managed to squeeze her head through the square, but when she attempted to pull her head back, it pushed the wool up and against her small horns, leaving her lodged in the square. She had a very round head that she was trying to squeeze through a very square hole. When I approached her, I easily pushed her wool down and, by tipping her head from right to left, dislodged her horns so that the rest of her head easily pulled back through the hole. She trotted back to the other sheep with her head gratefully pressing against my knee. Clients often try to work through difficult situations without realizing there is an easier way. A square peg simply won't fit through a round hole. Modify your approach until you find a way to make your plans work.

My financially conservative mind often keeps me up at night as I struggle to make difficult decisions. In 2009, shortly after my mother had died, our youngest daughter started researching dog breeds and requesting a puppy. I wasn't on board initially. We already had two dogs living in our house, and it was hard to imagine making room for another one. There was the cost. She had settled on a Bernese mountain dog, and the puppies were expensive. They were also large dogs prone to have health problems and short life spans, so there were veterinarian bills to think about. She strongly argued her case, agreeing to provide all the dog's care and pointing out that our other dogs were old and bonded with my husband and me. I was up for nights agonizing over the decision. Bear, the Bernese, came to live with us right before Christmas, and he immediately filled a huge hole in our lives that we didn't even know existed. We spent the first few weeks of his life carrying him around like a baby, admiring his enormous paws and beautiful coat. Our daughter adored him, and he became popular in town when they would be off together on their adventures. When she got older and was in college or working full-time, I became his doggie day care, and he would spend his days lying by my feet in the office while I worked. Clients would often look for him under my desk, and some would sit and stroke his fur while we discussed stressful situations. He seemed to soothe them. Bear spent a lot of time with me in the gardens, and I would cup the peonies in my hand for him to sniff. We would all laugh to see him out on his own, wandering down the driveway, shoving his huge nose into the peonies for a whiff of fragrance. He was a gentle giant loved by everyone that knew him. He passed away just a year ago, having outlived his anticipated life span, and my heart opens with the question about finding another Bernese every time I see a picture of him or remember his sweet face. Life with Bear was an adventure worth having, and he reminded all of us that in darker times, there were still flowers to smell.

> My client, Elizabeth, was going through an extremely messy divorce, and her attorney brought me on board for forensic accounting

services. Her husband had accumulated a bunch of rental properties and was attempting to hide the properties as well as the trail of rental income in the divorce proceedings. Elizabeth's attorney was determined to strip her husband of the rental properties in the divorce, which would provide Elizabeth with a steady stream of future rental income. Elizabeth came to me one day in a panic. She had been trying to explain to her attorney that she had no desire to own or manage rental properties. In fact, she hated the idea of being a rental property owner entirely. She didn't want the headache or the mess of having to deal with those properties. She was happy to let her husband keep them in exchange for the home that she lived in and loved, along with a cash settlement that her husband had already generously offered her. The divorce had been dragging on for the past few years, driven by her attorney's battle over the rental properties with Elizabeth's husband, who was determined to keep them. Elizabeth was tired of the process and ready for it to be over. Elizabeth's attorney wasn't listening to her client. Intellectually, she knew that the income stream from the rental properties would be a source of great future income for her client, but she was blind to what her client actually wanted. Ultimately, we had a meeting with all parties, and the attorney finally realized that her attempts to get the properties for her client were misguided. The divorce process wrapped up quickly, and Elizabeth and her husband got to keep the things that meant the most to them.

Working with clients requires me to push aside my own experience and make room for the client's needs. Therapists and other professionals can have transference issues when their own belief systems or ideals interfere with their ability to clearly direct a client toward the solution best for them. The same happens with friends or family members. These people make recommendations based on how the outcome affects them or on their own similar life experiences, and it can be difficult for these people to separate themselves enough from a situation to deliver sound advice.

Have faith in your own ability to process a situation and direct yourself to a positive outcome. You can absolutely solicit advice from friends, family, or professionals, weigh the pros and cons but remember to listen to your own heart and inner voice. Lead with your heart and then put in the work to make your choice a viable one. Opportunities will present themselves along your journey through life, and you will decide which path to follow. Once you've made the decision, be prepared to put in the work to make your dreams a reality. Be open to making changes to your plans if you hit obstacles and realize that not all paths will be a perfect fit. Modify or change your plans when needed. If you want to reap the harvest, you will need more than just luck and a promise to grow your seed.

- Have you listened to your heart when making a decision?

- Did it end up being a good or bad decision?

- What is your process for making decisions?

- Do you listen to your internal voice when making decisions?

Chapter 28
Be Humble and Kind

Kindness is like snow. It beautifies everything it covers.

—Kahlil Gibran

Recently, I made a colossal mistake and printed a twenty-seven thousand dollar check on the wrong blank check form, causing an overdraft in an account used for payroll. We were away on vacation, and obviously, in the craziness involved in getting ready to leave, I made a mistake. The payroll company was requesting a wire transfer to cover the balance overdrawn before they would allow us to process our next payroll. My first step was to phone our local bank and attempt to have them do a wire transfer. The call was routed to a service center, and their response was that they could not do the transfer based on a verbal conversation. I called the local branch directly and spoke to someone there that knew my business. I explained that I had made a huge mistake and apologized for the inconvenience of the request. She was happy to help, but bank policy wouldn't allow the transfer since I couldn't print and sign it. I then phoned the payroll company and spoke to a woman there that knew my business. Again, I explained my error and apologized for the mistake. They were happy to initiate the transfer on their end and run the necessary payroll. Experience has taught me that the best way to get results is to own your mistakes and get the people you need on board with wanting to help you. Making mistakes makes us all human, and owning them makes us relatable. Own your mistakes; treat people with respect, and most will do their best to help you fix the situation.

My client, Andrea, is a wealthy woman with a miserable disposition. She does her best to hide her wealth to maintain friendships in the community because she's afraid people won't like her if they know about her wealth. She treats everyone that does business with her horribly, and people talk about her constantly behind her back. She negotiates the cost of everything, from getting her hair colored to the price per gallon she pays for oil. Andrea always wants to get a deal. She makes demands of people's time but refuses to pay any additional costs. She buys her oil from a discount oil company and won't pay the premium for automatic delivery and then won't pay the technician to prime her boiler when she runs out of oil. "I buy oil from you. Isn't that enough?" she asks. A few years ago, her business was randomly audited by the state unemployment department. The agent contacted me directly since I prepared the returns, and my office forwarded the necessary documents and completed the audit. She refused to pay the invoice for the service, stating that it was not her error that her business was randomly selected for an audit. "The state should pay the bill," she declared. "Get it from them." Many businesses have put her on a "do not service" list. She manages a local business and has a hard time keeping employees. She bullies and intimidates the people unfortunate enough to take a job there. She believes that paying people entitles her to abuse them. She worries that her wealth is what drives people away but fails to see the connection between her lack of kindness and her lack of popularity within the community.

There is a saying that *you catch more bees with honey than you do with vinegar*. This saying rings so true. My first, second, and sometimes even third attempts always start with a positive approach, and rarely have there been situations that couldn't be resolved that were initiated with kindness. Owning your faults or failures in a situation goes a long way toward acknowledging your role in the problem and allows you to ask for help. Be humble enough to admit your mistakes and ask for help nicely. Most people, I have found, like to help. Let them.

Growing up, we had a special plate that we used for the cakes my mother made for our family birthdays. It was my mother's fanciest plate. A blue onion pattern on a milk glass plate sat on a small pedestal. One day while I washed the plate in hot sudsy water, the little pedestal fell off the plate. It was, I discovered, a simple custard bowl that some ingenious housewife had glued to the bottom of a plate. We continued to use that humble plate, and we never glued the pedestal back on. You see, it wasn't the pedestal that made the plate special. When I left home and started a family of my own, my mother gave me that plate for my own cakes. From the time my daughters were little to the days of the grandchildren that we celebrate now, that humble plate has continued to hold the cakes that make these days special; no fancy pedestal is needed.

Many years ago, my husband pointed out a negative trait I had that I wasn't aware of. When checking out of the grocery store, I was often distracted and didn't acknowledge the cashier or person bagging the groceries. I was disappointed in myself, recognized this characteristic to be true, and I didn't like this behavior in myself. I knew that when checking out, I was totally preoccupied with the grocery list running through my head, double-checking my mental list to see if I had forgotten something. It was easy to correct this behavior, and now I always make eye contact with the cashier and bagger and thank them both for their service. It takes only seconds out of my day to honor their efforts and let them know they are appreciated.

A family member I was once close to has always had a horrible habit of insulting people, utilizing sarcasm to disguise the insult as a joke or a helpful comment. Psychologically, I know that she has issues of inferiority and feels that by knocking someone else down, she elevates her own status. For example, she will compliment you on your outfit but say, "Hmmm, it looks a little too tight though. I'm wondering if you should have gotten it in a larger size." One night, after a few cocktails, she laughed as she told me about this funny thing she does where she insults people and that they aren't even smart enough to know she's insulting them because they think she's simply being helpful or making a joke. It was surprising to hear that she was that intentional in choosing to deliver hurtful comments. I responded back that I was smart enough to know I was being insulted every time she had done it to me but was simply choosing not to engage in her negativity. Her ensuing silence made me wonder if she was smart enough to know that other people were probably aware of her insults as well. Eventually, her barbed wire comments became too difficult to be around, and I moved on to other pastures with kinder fencing.

My mother was easily the kindest person I've ever met, and in her lifetime, she never had a negative thing to say about anyone she knew. She remembered everyone's birthdays and was generous with her gifting. We often joked that she spent most of the income from her postal job shopping for gifts for the people in her life. Sometimes, for fun, we would goad her to get a negative comment about someone out of her, but she was resolute in her defense of every single person she knew. There was a supervisor at the post office, Roberta, that seemed to have it in for my mother, and we suspected that she was jealous of my mother's popularity in the office. Roberta had few friends and was not well-liked. In any event, Roberta would initiate a conversation asking what plans my mother might have, and as soon as my mother revealed that she had plans to visit with her kids or grandkids or something else fun planned, Roberta would say what a shame since she needed my mother to work that particular day. Eventually, my mother got wise to her plans and learned not to share information with Roberta since she would inevitably have to end up working, and plans would have to be canceled. Shortly before she passed away, my mother was telling me about the people in her life and how lucky she had been to be so loved. She mentioned her nemesis, Roberta, and excused her behavior, saying, "You know, she just wasn't very loved by anyone." My mother came home from the hospital to die, and we set up the hospital bed on her porch so that she could watch the birds that came to feed outside the windows. For thirteen days, there was a steady stream of visitors as the people in my mother's life came to say goodbye. When she passed, the hall where we had her funeral was filled to capacity. My mother had spent her days spreading kindness and left this world well-loved.

In every transaction, we have the option of choosing how we treat the people with whom we are interacting. Be mindful of your words and thoughtful of the energy you share with others because negative energy will be remembered long after you have exited the room. Every single day, you can decide to meet the people in your life with kindness and generosity of spirit. Imagine a world where we all worked toward greeting each other with a smile and sending out messages of kindness and respect to the people we encountered in our days. Plant seeds of kindness wherever you wander, and you will be pleased with what you grow.

- How do you spread kindness in your days?

- Have you ever been less than kind and regretted it?

- Can you see a positive reaction when you deal with people with kindness?

Chapter 29
Listen to It

Isn't it amazing that so many of the people our culture idolizes are young actresses or musicians so young and inexperienced in life that they have little to draw upon? A few minutes of fame and they are in front of the camera, telling the people of the world how to live better lives. Young people don't know themselves yet and don't know the world well enough to be telling anyone how to live. I've harvested some of my best advice from people who have lived through many seasons and have the experiences to back the advice they yield. If I want help setting up my phone, Facebook, or iPad, I'll ask a young person, but when it comes to real life, I turn to the people that have a few years under their belts. Why do we continue to discount the people in our world that have the most experiences to draw from? Old people know a lot of shit. They can tell you how to find your way out of the woods, identify animals by their tracks, and tell the weather by looking at the clouds. They can tell you how to deal with difficult relationships based on the things they've experienced in their own lives. They are wise to the ways of the world. When we are younger, we think they're outdated and out of touch, but as we get older, we realize the value of the information they hold. Listen to them.

Embrace where you are in life, whatever season that might be. Appreciate the lines on your face and the knowledge you've collected from your journey through life. Difficulties that you've encountered along your path have formed you into the person you are today. Appreciate the gifts that these lessons have given you. Respect the wisdom you've learned along your journey through life, and know that the lines and the gray hair are the beauty marks you've earned along the way. There is value in all this. Listen to it.

Your heart has a voice of its own; don't stuff it down. Run the numbers, consult with friends and family, but remember to ask your heart what it wants. Sit quietly in the dark and feel with your heart. Ask the heart what it wants. Visualize yourself in different realities and look inside yourself to see how your heart feels in each situation. Your heart has desires. Slow your mind enough to listen to the whisperings of your heart.

When your head and your heart are aligned, you will hear another voice. This voice is intuition. When your intuition screams at you that a situation doesn't feel right or safe, listen to it. Pull deep inside yourself and ask in the deepest part of you how something feels. Ask yourself if something feels right, and listen to the voice that guides you. I keep a roster of almost six hundred clients, and repeatedly, thoughts of a certain client have entered my mind, only to have that client call with a question the very next day. Sometimes, I will recall a client I haven't heard from in years, only to hear from them the next day. That day, I was standing at the kitchen sink, washing vegetables, and my mother called with news from her doctor. My heart started pounding, my vision blurred, and I knew things were going to be bad before she even had the test results. Ten years ago, after suffering through two painful family deaths, I was standing in my bedroom window when a voice told me that soon, I would be a grandmother. I didn't know what that would entail, but I knew it would bring joy. The very next day, my daughter told me she was pregnant with our grandson. Knowing him has brought us all unimaginable joy. There was another voice, much more recent, that compelled me out of bed at night and demanded that I write this book. I listened to that voice, and yet another voice compelled you to pick up this book. A connection has been made. Where rhyme and reason intersect lies the voice of your intuition. This voice defies logic or explanation, but I've learned to listen to it. Your intuition is the powerful result of your freed mind and heart, providing you with an insight your mind alone can't deliver. Your intuition has a message to share. Listen to it.

Chapter 30
Tiny Seeds

> For a seed to achieve its greatest expression, it must come completely undone. The shell cracks, its insides come out, and everything changes. For someone who doesn't understand growth, it would look like complete destruction.
>
> —Cynthia Occelli

It is January in New England. In my little coastal farm town, the farmers have harvested their crops and filled their barns with a winter's worth of hay. The rains of last year's summer brought a wonderful harvest, and the farmers are happy. The dahlias have all been dug for the winter, and we are all pouring through seed catalogs with visions of this year's harvest dancing through our brains. My tax season will start in a few weeks, and more stories will be shared—stories of success and failures, changes in life that clients will be eager to share, and new plans for more changes will be made. On our farm, we will have lavender to harvest, and lambs will be born, perhaps even a mini donkey. The seasons will march on through yet another year, and once again, frost will settle on our woods and in our fields. We will raise and sell heritage turkeys again this year. And the tiny seeds I have sown will grow both in my gardens and in the world.

In 1988, my current husband and I will hire a talented young man to install a heating system in our home. I will move away to a small mountain town and return to Cape Cod nine years later, divorced with two young daughters, where I will purchase a home.

On a cold fall night, the furnace will break down, and I will find that talented man again. He will fix the heat in our home, and he will remember me, from so many years ago, as the young woman with a young baby who reminded him of the girl in the latest James Bond movie. As a mother, I will choose that man to help me raise my daughters, only to find that in choosing him for them, I have chosen the right man for myself as well. Tiny seeds planted nine years ago will finally germinate and push their way through the darkness to the light.

Years later and after your family has suffered the devastating loss of your own mother, you will discover that another kind of seed has been planted. This amazing tiny seed will make you a grandmother, and you will enter an amazing new season in your life. Your daughter will become the mother she needs to be to give that seed the most amazing life, and joy will grow again where darkness once lived.

You will see glimpses of your mother again, living in the lives your children grow. They will create homes that resemble hers, and together, you will pick blueberries and bake pies with the same graceful flute on the edges. More grandchildren will come, and you will see her smile, her eyes and hear laughter reminiscent of hers. Your house and heart will be full. The tiny seeds from one generation will be saved, planted, and will grow again in the lives of your children and grandchildren.

One day, your brother will call, and you will return to your childhood home to collect your baby book that's been discovered there among the rafters. Inside, you will find locks of your baby hair and memories of your birth. This book, dusty and more than fifty years old, will contain a secret buried in its back cover, and the identity of your real father, long wondered about, will be revealed. You will sigh and move on with this discovery knowing that it never really mattered. Tiny seed planted so many years ago, you were always whole.

The winter will find you in a mountain cabin, and you will revisit the paths and trails where your parents hiked, snowshoed, and strapped on their skis. You will make memories of your own and brave the cold, for there are stories that will need to be told. You will sit and write, the fire will burn, and you will open your heart and let lose all the stories and ideas your mind is busting with, scattering those tiny seeds into the wind for them to grow wherever they might land.

And if you're reading this book, the dream of a lifetime, built on many seasons of hard work, and stories shared, then you know that dreams can come true. For tiny seeds sown into fertile soil are the things upon which dreams are built.

Conclusion

Our season here together is coming to an end, and my, what a journey it has been. Beautiful reader, I started this book as a gift to you, but I have discovered so many gifts of my own along the way. That makes the best kind of gift, I think. It is the unexpected gift of the memories we uncover when we go through old photos, your mother's voice you hear in your head when you read through her journals kept in a bedside drawer, or perhaps the memories we hold in our minds and dust off from time to time when we sit and write. This book was like that for me.

Since childhood, I have loved to read, often rereading favorite books and collections of books by certain authors over and over again. Books sit in bookcases like old friends, and tracing my fingers along their spines will bring back fond memories of the stories held within their bindings. I have also always loved meeting with clients and listening to their stories, and I have pushed those stories away to corners of my mind, like a collection of precious seeds, until someday, I would find the time to share them. Blending this love of books and stories of all the clients I have known was always my dream. The fact that you are reading this book has made you a part of that dream, and I am grateful for that.

Listening to clients tell their stories and sharing those stories with other clients was always a way to make people feel as though they weren't alone. It helped them to know that other people were walking the same path, learning the same lessons, and growing in the same directions. As I learned from the stories of the clients I had known, so, too, did the clients I shared these stories with. I levied advice not only based on the books I had read and my own experience but also based on the stories and lives of my clients building paths to success. Seeing clients years later who recounted their success based on the stories or advice I had shared encouraged me to keep listening, learning, growing, and sharing.

The past two years of COVID have physically separated me from clients, but we have still found ways to connect through phone, email, Zoom, and appointments when we can schedule them. My work as an enrolled agent, licensed by the Internal Revenue Service, has allowed me to represent clients in cases of audits, collections, and appeals, and I specialize in working with non-filers and self-employed people. It has always made for interesting days. Doing this type of work takes you deep into a client's financial life and opens many doors into other areas of their lives. The clients I work with have always been eager to share their stories. Collaborating with them has always been about building relationships, and I have been fortunate to work with kind and amazing people over many years. They are all very dear to me.

In drafting this book, I connected the words and stories to the things I love most in life. My love of animals, gardening, and trees made the writing flow effortlessly, and the parallels between growing a successful life and planting seeds made for an easy and natural connection. Having animals on our farm provides us with an easy stream of humor and lightness, and my hope is that this is carried through in my writing. It's impossible not to be in a good mood in the morning after feeding the sheep, donkeys, and birds on our farm. We often just stand and laugh at the antics of our barnyard ducks and Tom, the large turkey, who manages all the other barnyard birds.

My hope is that I've planted seeds in the garden of your soul and that there will be a harvest for you to reap. Plant in faith and harvest with good work. In a few months, the frost will be out of the ground. Will you plant some of those seeds that I have blown your way?

Once again, dusk has settled into the forest outside the windows of this mountain cabin, and snow is falling softly. Life is calling to us both. Go plant something beautiful!

About the Author

Sherri Mahoney has owned an accounting practice, Taxing Matters, since 1987. Sherri is an enrolled agent (enrolled agents are the only federal licensed tax preparer who also have unlimited rights to represent taxpayers before the IRS). With years of experience behind her, Sherri has presented seminars for small business owners, spoken on local radio programs, and written articles for publications on life, taxes, and financial issues. She lives on a small family farm in Westport with her husband, where they grow lavender and raise sheep, peacocks, donkeys, and an assortment of barnyard birds.